CONTINUOUS IMPROVEMENT

TOOLS IN EDUCATION
VOLUME 1

A Practical Guide
To Achieving Quality Results

Richard Y. Chang, Ph.D.
Doug Dalziel

American Productivity & Quality Center
Education Initiative
Houston, Texas

Richard Chang Associates, Inc.
Publications Division
Irvine, California

CONTINUOUS IMPROVEMENT TOOLS IN EDUCATION
VOLUME 1

A Practical Guide To Achieving Quality Results

Richard Y. Chang, Ph.D.
Doug Dalziel

Originally published as *Continuous Improvement Tools, Volume 1*
        By Richard Y. Chang and Matthew E. Niedzwiecki
© 1993, Richard Chang Associates, Inc.

Names used in this book are purely hypothetical and are not intended to suggest or depict actual names of persons or organizations.

© 1999, Richard Chang Associates, Inc.
15265 Alton Parkway, Suite 300
Irvine, CA 92618

Printed in the United States of America

First Printing: Education Version, November 1999
ISBN 1-883553-14-8 (Volume 1)
ISBN 1-883553-19-9 (2-Volume Set)

Library of Congress Catalog Card Number
99-75224

Distributed by:
American Productivity & Quality Center
123 North Post Oak Lane
Houston, TX 77024-7797
(800) 776-9676 • Fax (713) 681-8578
www.apqc.org

PREFACE

The 1990's presented individuals and educational institutions with some very difficult challenges to face and overcome. So who will have the advantage as we move beyond the year 2000?

The advantage will belong to those with a commitment to continuous, innovative learning. It will mean using systems and processes *(not unaligned and random acts of improvement)* in a new, dynamic way in education. With this paradigm shift before us, the American Productivity & Quality Center *(APQC)* has partnered with Richard Chang Associates, Inc. to bring you the *APQC Education Series.*

The future *"learning needs"* expressed by our education clients, and other potential customers, are reflected in the *APQC Education Series.* These guidebooks are designed to provide you with proven, *"real-world"* tips, tools, and techniques—on a wide range of subjects—that you can apply in the education workplace and/or on a personal level immediately.

Once you've had a chance to benefit from the *APQC Education Series,* please share your feedback with us. We've included a brief *Evaluation And Feedback Form* at the end of the guidebook that you can fax to us at (713) 681-8578.

With your feedback, we can continuously improve the resources we are providing and together improve the education of this and future generations.

Wishing you success,

C. Jackson Grayson, Jr.
Chairman
American Productivity & Quality Center

Acknowledgments

APQC Founder:

C. Jackson Grayson, Jr. is founder and chairman of the American Productivity & Quality Center *(APQC)* in Houston, Texas—a nonprofit organization focused on helping all organizations improve. Under Grayson's direction, APQC has been recognized as a leader in organizational improvement through benchmarking, process improvement, knowledge management, and quality and productivity tools. The former chairman of President Nixon's Price Commission, Grayson also served as dean of two business schools, Tulane University and Southern Methodist University, where he became known for instituting innovations in business education.

Authors:

Richard Y. Chang, Ph.D. is CEO of Richard Chang Associates, Inc., a performance improvement consulting, training, and publishing firm headquartered in Irvine, California. He has consulted to a wide variety of private, public, educational, and not-for-profit organizations; served as faculty for several Universities and Community Colleges; and provided leadership to further Business-Education-Government partnerships. With a Ph.D. in Industrial/Organizational Psychology, Dr. Chang has authored over twenty books addressing a variety of organizational and personal development topics, served as Chair of the Board for the American Society for Training and Development *(ASTD)*, and held the position of Judge for the Malcolm Baldrige National Quality Award.

Doug Dalziel, Senior Instructional Designer for Richard Chang Associates, Inc., is a skilled program designer, consultant, and educator. His extensive background and areas of expertise include total quality management, performance management, team building, customer focus, and learning systems design.

The authors would like to acknowledge the support of the entire team of professionals at Richard Chang Associates, Inc. for their contribution to the guidebook development process. In addition, special thanks are extended to the staff of APQC and the many clients who have helped us shape the practical ideas and proven methods shared in this guidebook.

Editors:	Jennifer Merta, Sarah Gensler, and Pamela Wade
Reviewers:	Gretchen Gemeinhardt and Ruth Stingley
Graphic Layout:	Rich Baisner and Melissa Zirretta
Cover Design:	Dena Putnam and Dottie Snyder

TABLE OF CONTENTS

> *"The single most destructive force in the move to improving the quality of American organizations today is the lack of commitment and understanding of how to make quality happen on the job."*
>
> Anonymous

INTRODUCTION

Total quality management. You've heard about it. You've seen much written about it. You may even be applying the concepts *(successfully or not so successfully)* right now in your school. Education's quality revolution is upon us, and unlike some of the other school improvement initiatives you may have been through…this one's here to stay!

Why Read This Guidebook?

In today's school environment, things seem to change daily *(or hourly, in some cases)*! How do you keep up? The answer: Everyone in your district, from the superintendent to the teacher, must be committed to continuously improving all that he or she does to establish quality schools.

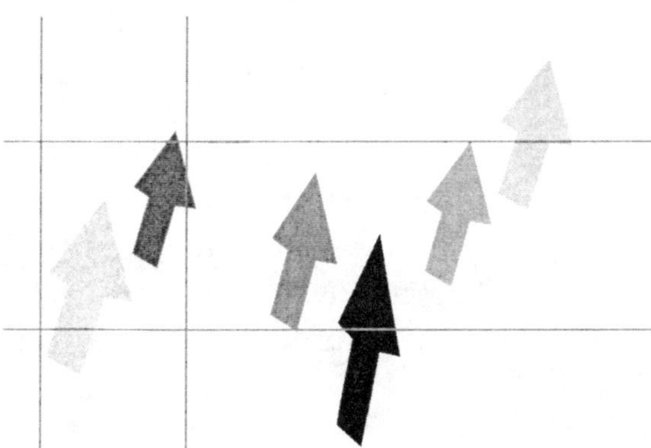

The question that has haunted organizations and individuals attempting to implement school improvement plans over the years still rings loud and clear: *"What can we do to improve our schools and the education of our students?"*

Often, the responsibility for improvement gets pushed up, down, and sideways in schools. From the superintendent's office to the classroom, you can hear these echoing words: *"I can't do anything about it!"* But, you can!

Who Should Read This Guidebook?

You should; and through it, you can do something to make quality happen! The tools and techniques presented in this guidebook offer a common sense approach that will help you *(as a teacher, principal, superintendent, etc.)* not only begin, but also sustain, quality-improvement efforts *(e.g., process improvement, problem-solving teams, instructional teams, etc.)* already in place in your school.

When And How To Use This Guidebook

You may use and reference this guidebook during meetings, while working on teams, or anytime you have a question about which *"quality tool"* to use and/or how to use it.

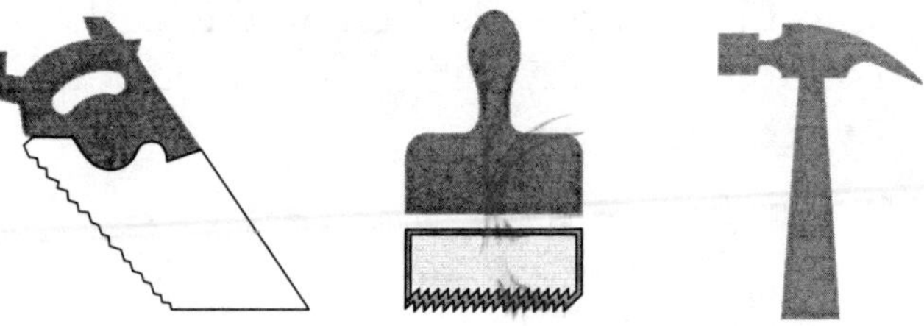

Continuous Improvement Tools In Education, Volume 1 contains step-by-step instructions along with real-life examples. Included are seven basic—yet popular and effective—quality tools: Brainstorming, Affinity Diagram, Matrix Diagram, Force Field Diagram, Cause And Effect Diagram, Criteria Rating Form, and the Check Sheet.

When deciding which tool to use for your situation, take a moment to look at the Selection Matrix on the next page. Whether you need a tool for planning, analysis, or interpretation—you'll find these tools useful, practical, and easy to adapt for your own purposes.

At the end of each chapter, you'll find a worksheet to jot down ideas for using the specific tool in your work as an educator. In addition, there are worksheets and blank reproducible forms in the Appendix for you to use on the job. Write in this guidebook, fold the pages, get it dirty, but don't let it sit on your shelf!

Continuous Improvement Tools In Education: Selection Matrix

	USE → Planning	Analysis	Interpretation	Team	Individual
VOLUME 1					
Brainstorming	X	X		X	
Affinity Diagram	X	X		X	
Matrix Diagram	X			X	X
Force Field Diagram		X		X	
Cause and Effect		X		X	
Criteria Rating	X		X	X	X
Check Sheet		X	X		X
VOLUME 2					
Tree Diagram	X			X	
Pareto Chart			X		X
Sequence Flow Chart	X	X		X	X
Process Flow Chart	X	X		X	X
Scatter Diagram			X		X
Run Chart		X	X		X
Control Chart		X	X		X
Histogram		X	X	X	X

Note: In Volume 2, tools and techniques such as Pareto Charting, Process And Sequence Flowcharting, Scatter Diagrams, Run/Control Charts, and the Tree Diagram are discussed in detail.

BRAINSTORMING

Brainstorming is a planning tool you can use to tap the creativity of a group. Education teams and departments should use Brainstorming when:

- 👉 **Determining possible causes and/or solutions to problems**

- 👉 **Planning out the steps of a project**

- 👉 **Deciding which problem *(or improvement opportunity)* to work on**

Teams often use Brainstorming as a consensus-building tool, and in situations where they need to generate a large number of ideas.

The two key steps to Brainstorming are:

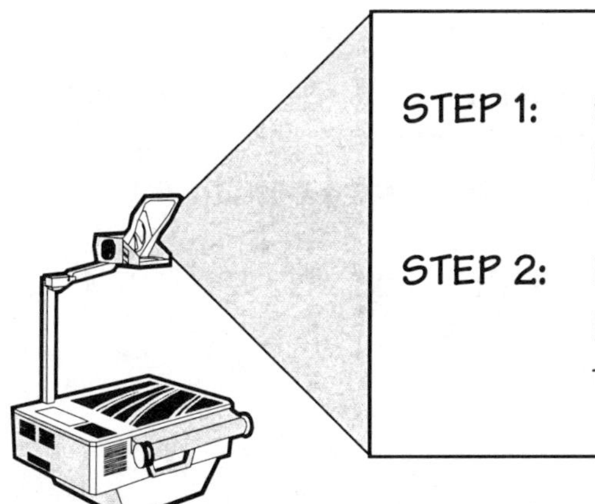

Let's look at an example of how Brainstorming works in the school environment—in this case, it's a problem-solving team at South High School.

Pat, the Assistant Principal of Instruction and the leader ...

of a problem-solving team at South High, thought the team needed a jump-start to come up with new ideas on how to improve the performance of failing and marginal students.

Currently, the only option is for students to attend summer school or repeat a course.

Pat started the session off by saying, *"Let's try to brainstorm some new ideas."* Ignoring the usual moans and grumbling about trying new methods, Pat launched into the Brainstorming session....

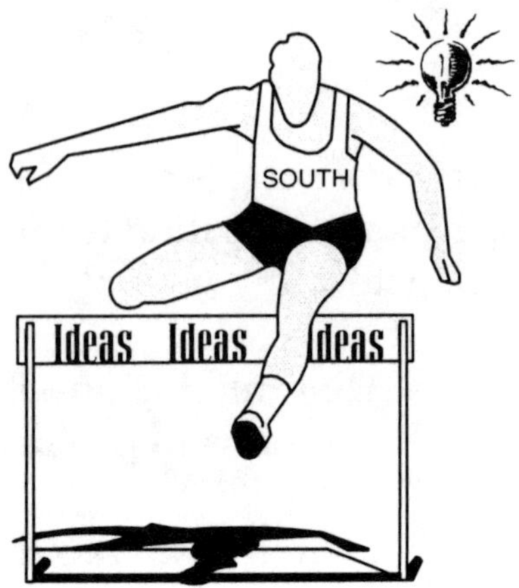

Step 1: Start The Brainstorming Session

➤ Provide a time limit for the session. Generally, 30 minutes is sufficient.

➤ Identify one or more Recorders. The Recorder's job is to write all ideas down *(where everyone can see them, such as on a flip chart or overhead transparency)* as they are voiced.

➤ Establish the ground rules *(see Diagram # 1).*

The problem-solving team decided ...

to brainstorm for 30 minutes. Denise agreed to be the Recorder. As Denise stood at the flip chart, armed with three different-colored markers and prepared to use her charting skills, Pat reminded the team not to criticize even the most outrageous ideas. Pat hoped they'd generate at least 30 ideas during the 30-minute session....

GROUND RULES

⇨ Don't edit what is said and remember not to criticize ideas.

⇨ Go for quantity of ideas at this point; narrow down the list later.

⇨ Encourage wild or exaggerated ideas (creativity is the key).

⇨ Build on the ideas of others (e.g., one member might say something that "sparks" another member's idea).

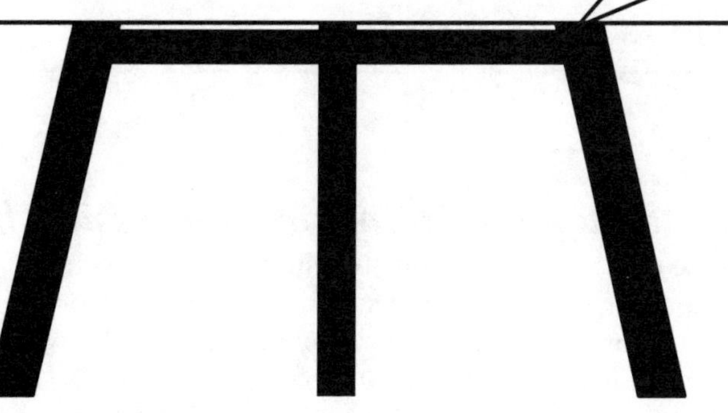

Diagram # 1 - Ground Rules

Step 2: Determine The Type Of Brainstorming Method To Use

Choose either the **freewheeling** or **round robin** method of Brainstorming.

Pat began the team's Brainstorming session by ...

offering an idea that Denise promptly listed on the flip chart. After that, some more team members chimed in with ideas, and then silence fell over the group. Pat thought, *"How can we be out of ideas already?"* After a few moments, Pat suggested the team switch gears and use the round-robin approach, explaining that each person around the table would consecutively offer an idea, or pass to the next person.

This approach was more effective, and soon the members were back to *"shouting out"* ideas. Denise even had trouble keeping up, since the ideas were coming so fast. Ted volunteered to help record....

Decide On Next Steps

You know it's time to end your Brainstorming session when:

After about half an hour ...

the team ran out of ideas. Pat announced, *"last call for ideas"* Ted mischievously replied, *"Oh no, I want to go for another hour!"* Everyone laughed, and the team knew the rag had been rung dry. Pat thanked all the participants for their enthusiasm, and Denise and Ted for their willingness to get sore hands as Recorders. The team agreed to wait until the following week to prioritize their ideas and decide on a starting point in their problem-solving process.

After you've finished Brainstorming:

➠ Prioritize your ideas to help you decide where to start.

➠ Sort large amounts of information according to common themes *(see the Affinity Diagram in the next chapter).*

➠ Remember, Brainstorming is based on people's opinions, so you may need to gather data to support or prove ideas.

In summary, use Brainstorming when:

☑ You want to determine possible causes and/or solutions to problems. *(Brainstorming helps your team generate a large quantity of ideas.)*

☑ Planning out the steps of a project. *(Although not the primary use of this tool, Brainstorming can be used to help identify the different steps in implementing a project.)*

☑ Deciding which problem *(or improvement opportunity)* to work on. *(You can use Brainstorming in any situation where many ideas need to be generated in a relatively short period of time.)*

☑ You want to include all opinions. *(Round-Robin Brainstorming helps ensure equal participation in an idea-generating session.)*

CHAPTER TWO WORKSHEET:
BRAINSTORMING—IDEAS FOR USE

1. List some specific opportunities you have to use Brainstorming.

____

____

____

____

____

____

2. Which method will work best in the situations you listed, and why?

☐ Freewheeling. Why?

____

____

____

____

____

____

☐ Round Robin. Why?

____

____

____

____

____

3. What kinds of ground rules should be used for the situations you listed in question #1?

☐ No judging, evaluating or criticizing

☐ Go for quantity

☐ Be creative

☐ Build on ideas

☐ Other: _______________________________________

____

☐ Other: _______________________________________

____

AFFINITY DIAGRAM

You should use the Affinity Diagram as a planning tool when you want to:

- **Add structure to a large or complicated issue**

- **Break down a complicated issue into easy-to-understand categories**

- **Gain agreement on an issue or situation**

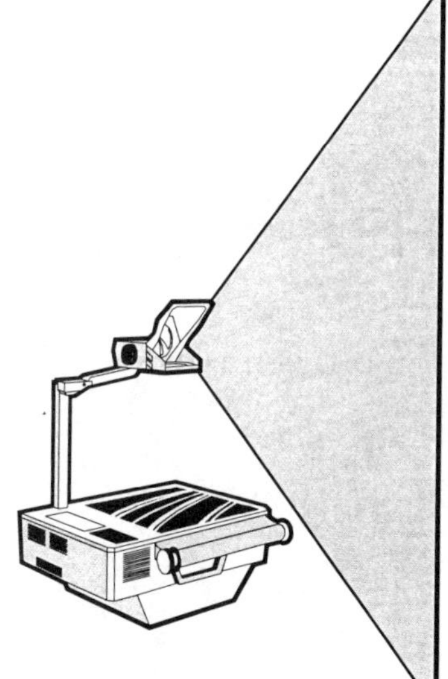

In the following example, a team—that has representation from both education and business—uses the Affinity Diagram to help organize a complex educational issue.

Anthony is the Assistant District Superintendent and the leader ...

of a team composed of district personnel and several representatives from local businesses. The team's task is to come up with ideas of how businesses can help students prepare for life after graduation.

All members agree that the partnership is mutually beneficial. Schools will be able to better prepare students for the real world, and businesses will someday have a local pool of talent from which to draw.

Anthony has seen the Affinity Diagram used in situations where large amounts of data need to be organized. *"Well,"* he decided, *"this is certainly a situation where a tool like that could be helpful...."*

Step 1: State The Issue Or Problem To Be Worked On

At the start of your Affinity session:

➡ Provide a time limit for the session. Generally, 45 to 60 minutes is sufficient.

➡ Start with a clear, objective problem or goal statement that everyone agrees to.

After the team ...

(including the representatives from local businesses) filed in, Anthony asked all those present to introduce themselves. He announced the team's goal *(which he had written on a flip chart)*. He also said the meeting would last about an hour....

Step 2: Generate Ideas For The Issue In Question

➤ Each participant should think of ideas and write them on index cards, sticky notes, or have a Recorder write them on a flip chart.

Note: The advantage of using the flip chart is that everyone can see the ideas and build from them. See the previous chapter for Brainstorming ground rules. The disadvantage of this technique is that group members may be intimidated by this process and not participate.

➤ The idea statements should be concisely listed in one to three words. One idea should be used per card or sticky note.

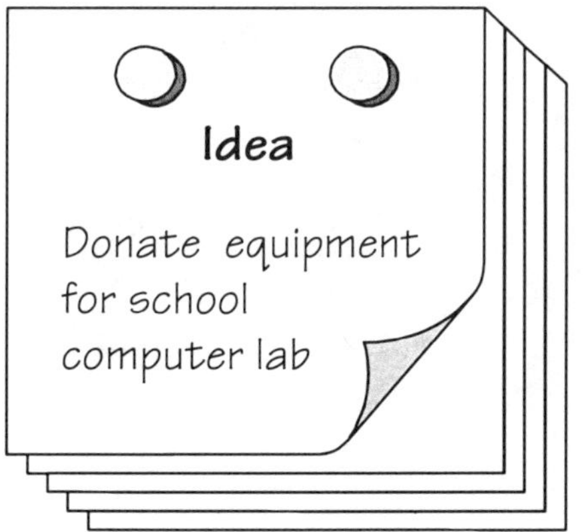

Anthony handed a stack of sticky notes ...

to each participant and asked them to write their thoughts about what local businesses can do to help schools in the district. He reminded them to write only one idea on each sticky note. The team had some trouble getting started, but after a couple of minutes, all were busily writing. Anthony gave the team 15 minutes to complete this part of the exercise....

Step 3: Collect The Cards Or Sticky Notes

➠ Collect the cards *(or sticky notes)*, mix them up and then spread them out *(or stick them)* on a flat surface.

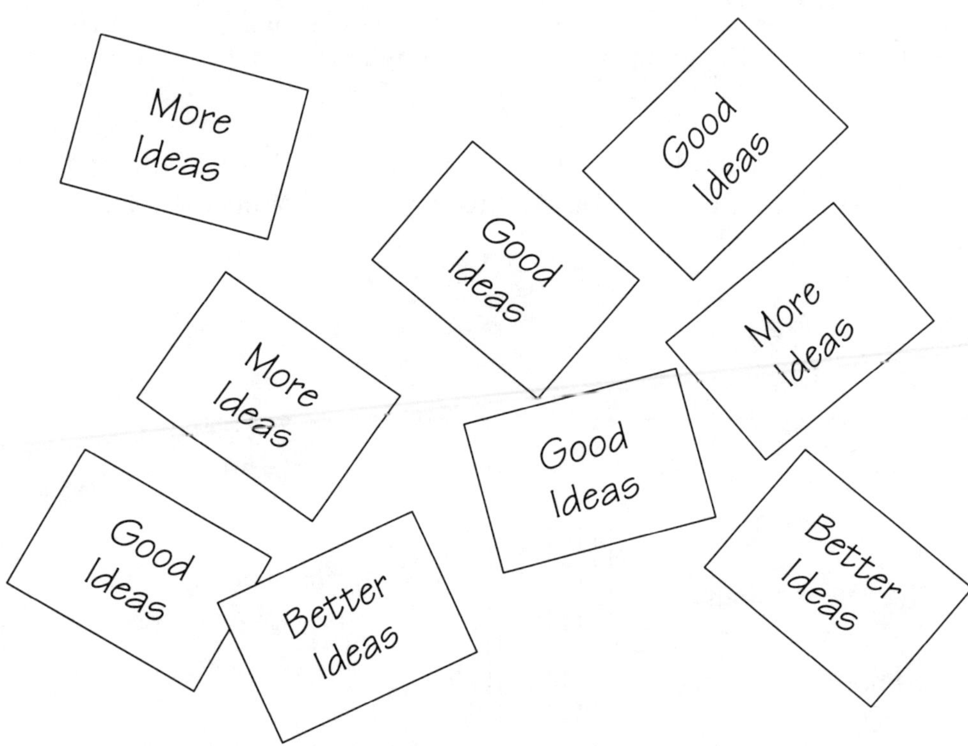

Anthony called "time," ...

and collected the ideas from the participants. He mixed them up before sticking them on the wall to ensure the ideas would remain anonymous. That way no bias would be involved—all ideas would be treated equally....

Step 4: Arrange The Cards Or Sticky Notes Into Related Groups

➤ All participants should pick out cards *(or sticky notes)* that list related ideas and set them aside. Repeat this until all of the cards *(or sticky notes)* have been placed in groupings.

Note: Don't force cards *(or sticky notes)* into groupings. There may be only one card *(or sticky note)* per grouping. In some cases you may decide not to use an idea at all *(e.g., some ideas may be duplicates).*

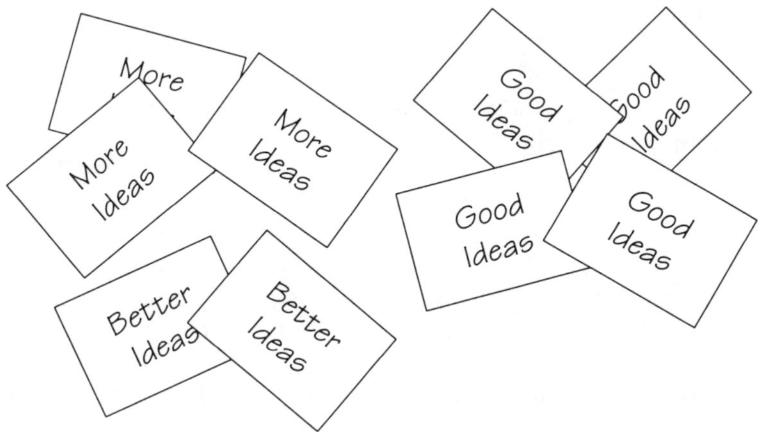

Diagram # 2 - Ideas arranged by related group

➤ This process should take about 15 minutes and works best when conversation between participants is not allowed. This encourages freethinking and discourages arguments over placement of cards *(or sticky notes).*

After Anthony stuck all the sticky notes to the wall, ...

he asked the team to arrange the ideas into related groups *(see Diagram # 2)*. Anthony asked that this task be done in silence, so no one would be influenced by any other team member. As the participants began moving sticky notes around, it looked as though the ideas were being separated into four major groups....

Step 5: Create A Title Or Heading For Each Group

➤ Develop a title or heading that best describes the theme of each group of cards *(or sticky notes)*.

➤ Headings should be short *(one to three words)* and describe the main theme/focus of the group it represents.

➤ To help you see additional relationships, place groups that are similar next to each other.

➤ If groups are very similar, you can combine two or more groups to create one large group under a new title or heading.

➤ Continue this process until your team agrees on the grouping of cards.

After discussing the idea groupings …

for 15 minutes, it became obvious to the participants that four distinct categories of *"how businesses can assist schools"* had emerged. The categories were internships, after-school jobs, guest instructors, and career fairs. The remaining two sticky notes were grouped in a *"miscellaneous"* category *(see Diagram # 3)*.…

INTERNSHIPS	AFTER-SCHOOL JOBS	GUEST INSTRUCTORS	CAREER FAIRS	MISCELLANEOUS
Idea Idea	Idea Idea	Idea Idea	Idea Idea	Idea Idea
Idea	Idea Idea	Idea Idea	Idea Idea	
	Idea		Idea Idea	

Diagram # 3 - Group the ideas and name each group

Decide On Next Steps

You know it's time to end the Affinity Diagram session when:

Remember that the process of completing the Affinity Diagram is an ongoing one. It is likely that you will modify or change your diagram.

It appeared the partnership ...

between the district and local businesses was on the right track. Anthony was in seventh heaven. He was thrilled to see the number of things local businesses could do to support the district's schools.

Anthony asked Dale to circulate the final Affinity Diagram among district officials on Monday, for their feedback and input. He thanked the team for participating in the process. Then, he scheduled a team follow-up meeting to discuss any changes to the Affinity Diagram and to map out their next steps.

In summary, use the Affinity Diagram when:

☑ You want to add structure when handling a large or complicated issue. *(The Affinity Diagram is a structured method of Brainstorming that you can use for larger, more complex activities such as developing a mission statement or a vision statement.)*

☑ You want to break down a complicated issue into easy-to-understand categories. *(An issue or problem may have several sub-issues, or may be so large that it needs to be broken down into more manageable pieces.)*

☑ You want to gain agreement on an issue or situation. *(When ideas are brainstormed individually, the Affinity Diagram is a useful tool to ensure that all team members have an equal voice.)*

CHAPTER THREE WORKSHEET:
AFFINITY DIAGRAM—IDEAS FOR USE

1. List some specific opportunities you have to use the Affinity Diagram.

____

____

____

____

____

____

2. What advantages or benefits of the Affinity Diagram would you describe to a team using it for the first time?

____

____

____

____

____

MATRIX DIAGRAM

The Matrix Diagram is a planning tool that can help you to organize large groups of tasks and responsibilities.

Note: There are many types of Matrix Diagrams. We will only be looking at the L-Shaped Diagram.

Use the Matrix Diagram to:

- **Match tasks with the individuals, departments, or functions completing them**

- **Show a relationship between a task and the responsible person, department, or function**

- **Rate the strength of that relationship**

- **Assign accountability and plan actions**

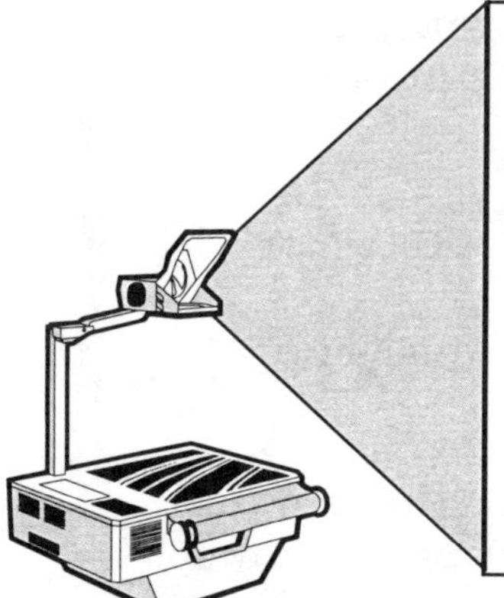

The example that follows illustrates a typical use of a Matrix Diagram in an education setting.

> ### *Kelsey, a seasoned teacher at Central Middle School ...*
>
> volunteered to lead a team responsible for implementing an orientation program for new teachers.
>
> Kelsey assembled a team of five teachers *(who would implement the program)* from different disciplines to work on this project....

Step 1: Prepare For The Matrix Diagram Session

At the start of your Matrix Diagram session:

➤ Create a flip chart or an overhead transparency of a Matrix Diagram *(see Diagram # 4)*.

➤ Provide a time limit for the session. Generally, 45 to 60 minutes is sufficient.

➤ Identify a Recorder. The job of the Recorder is to write down tasks *(on a flip chart or overhead transparency)*, responsible individuals and/or departments, and the strength of the relationship.

> ### *Kelsey called a meeting ...*
>
> to clarify the team's mission and to decide how to tackle the project at hand. Since the process had the potential to be complicated, Kelsey suggested using the Matrix Diagram. Kelsey explained that the Matrix Diagram would help them identify the tasks and responsibilities needed to complete the project. After drawing the matrix on a flip chart, Kelsey asked Liam to be the Recorder....

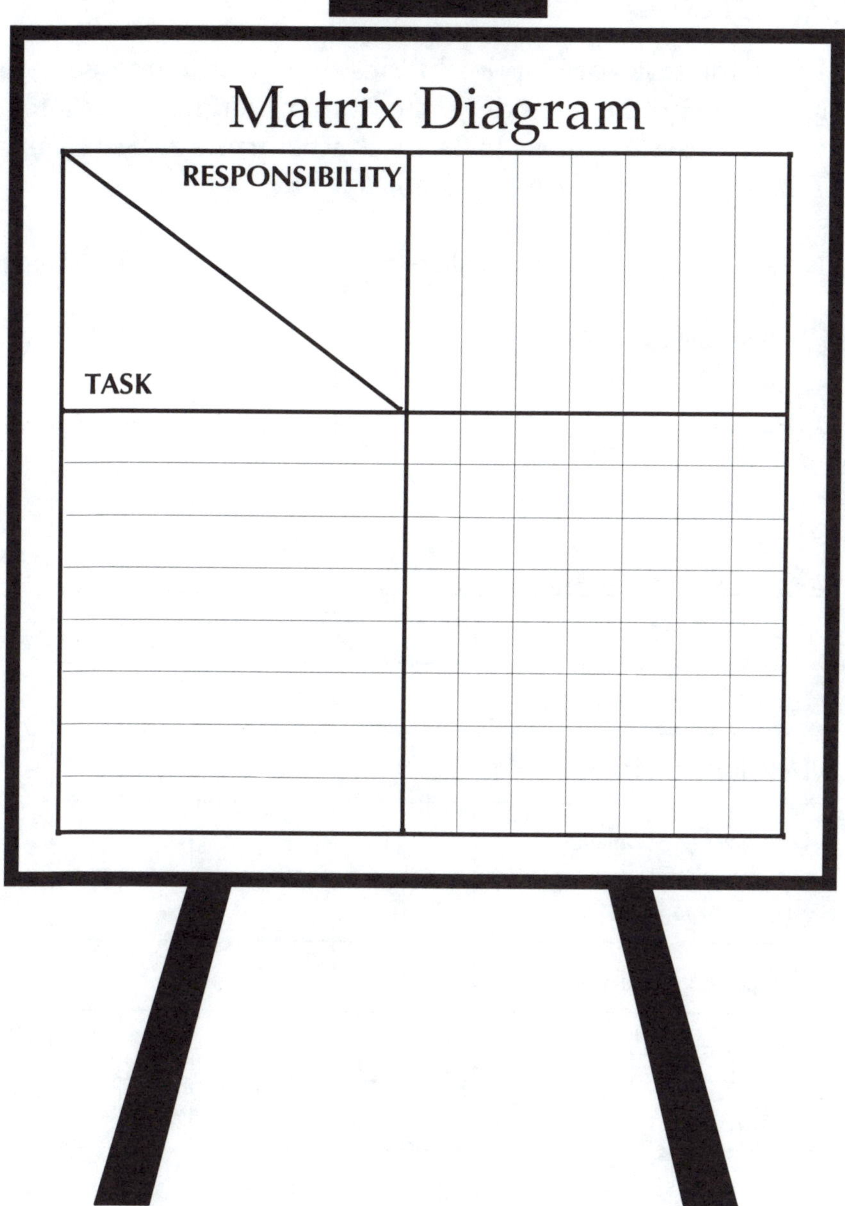

Diagram # 4 - The L-Shaped Matrix Diagram

Step 2: Agree On Tasks

➠ Write the tasks or responsibilities that your team needs to complete on the left side of the Matrix Diagram. As a team, you can identify these tasks by Brainstorming. *(See Chapter Two for the ground rules of Brainstorming.)*

Note: The tasks and responsibilities don't have to be in sequential order.

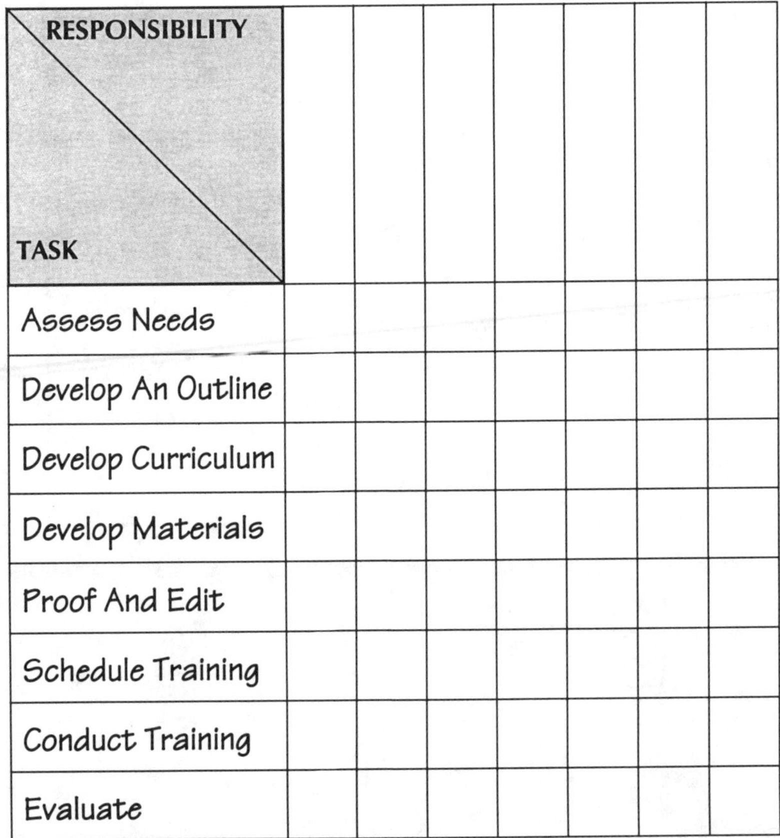

Diagram # 5 - Record the tasks

Kelsey asked the team to brainstorm a list of tasks ...

that they needed to complete in order to implement the orientation program for new teachers. The team decided on eight major tasks: assess needs, develop an outline, develop curriculum, develop materials, proof and edit materials, schedule training, conduct training, and evaluate training. Liam recorded all the responses on the left side of the Matrix Diagram *(see Diagram # 5)....*

Step 3: Record Responsibilities

⟹ Along the top of the Matrix Diagram, list the various individuals, departments, and/or suppliers that will complete the listed tasks or responsibilities.

After agreeing on the tasks,...

the team started to fill in the top of the Matrix Diagram with those who would be involved in the project. Each team member was listed—as were the school department heads, who would assist in the needs assessment, and the office staff, who would supply the training schedule. Once again, Liam filled out the information on the Matrix Diagram *(see Diagram # 6)*....

RESPONSIBILITY / TASK	Kelsey	Liam	Saida	Maria	Juan	Dept. Heads	Office Staff
Assess Needs							
Develop An Outline							
Develop Curriculum							
Develop Materials							
Proof And Edit							
Schedule Training							
Conduct Training							
Evaluate							

Diagram # 6 - Record the responsibilities

Step 4: Rate Each Intersection

➠ For each intersection of a task and an individual, department, or supplier, assign a *"strength"* rating using the following symbols:

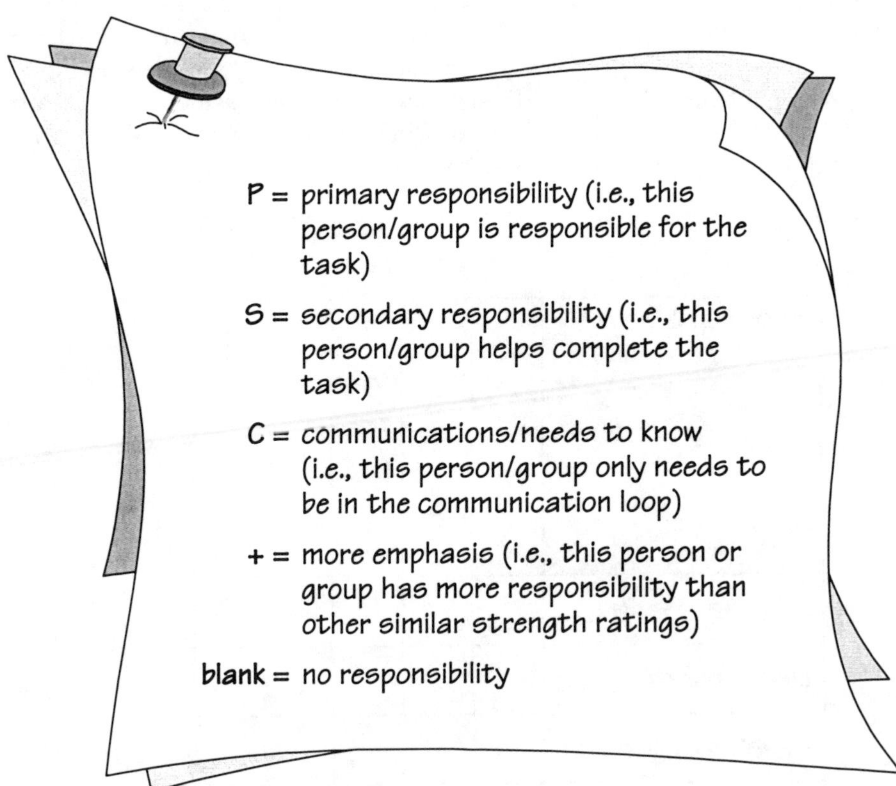

➠ Remember, each task must have one *(and only one)* rating of *"primary responsibility,"* since this indicates ownership of the task. The *"more emphasis"* rating is used to indicate a difference between two similar *"strength"* ratings (*i.e., if more than one person has two secondary responsibilities for a task, one might be labeled with a "+" for more emphasis*).

TASK \ RESPONSIBILITY	Kelsey	Liam	Saida	Maria	Juan	Dept. Heads	Office Staff
Assess Needs	C	P	S			S	
Develop An Outline	P	S+	C		S		
Develop Curriculum	P	S+	C				
Develop Materials			S	P	C		
Proof And Edit			S	P	S		
Schedule Training	C						P
Conduct Training	S	S	P	C			
Evaluate		C			P	S	

Diagram # 7 - Assign strength rating

Kelsey directed the attention ...

of the team members to the Matrix Diagram on the flip chart. Kelsey told them the next step was to assign a strength rating for each intersection of task and individual/department/supplier responsibility.

Liam volunteered to take the primary responsibility of assessing new teacher needs with the help of the department heads from mathematics, English, and social studies. Saida volunteered to help Liam, so Saida received an "S," as did the department heads. A "C" was placed in the Assess Needs box next to Kelsey's name. Kelsey asked to be in the *"communication loop"* and could then be responsible for developing a training outline from the needs assessment results. The rest of the intersection in Row 1 were left blank....

Decide On Next Steps

You know it's time to end the Matrix Diagram session when:

⇨ All tasks have been identified

⇨ All individuals, groups, and supplies needed to carry out the tasks have been identified

⇨ Each intersection on the matrix has been rated

⇨ Action assignments have been made (i.e., communicate responsibilities, clarify responsibilities, etc.)

⇨ You have thanked the participants

After the team had rated all the intersections, ...

they reviewed the matrix to make sure that the assignments made sense and that everyone had the time to carry out the tasks. The team then clarified exactly what each member would be doing and set the first action assignments.

Kelsey thanked Liam, the Recorder, and called for another meeting the following Wednesday to review progress and make any necessary changes in responsibilities. Kelsey then thanked the rest of the team members and adjourned the meeting, confident that everything needed to complete the project would be taken care of and that everyone was clear on who was responsible for what.

In summary, use the Matrix Diagram when:

☑ You want to match tasks with the individuals, departments, or functions completing them. *(Often when planning, we forget or omit the actual writing of the plan. The Matrix Diagram forces team members to match tasks with the individuals, departments, or functions completing them.)*

☑ You need to show a relationship between a task and the responsible person, department, or function. *(The Matrix Diagram should become a working plan that shows every implementation step and the person(s) responsible.)*

☑ You want to assign accountability and plan actions. *(Reviewing the Matrix Diagram periodically will help to hold people accountable to the plan of action.)*

CHAPTER FOUR WORKSHEET: MATRIX DIAGRAM—IDEAS FOR USE

1. List the specific opportunities you have to use a Matrix Diagram.

____

____

____

____

____

____

____

2. Of the following reasons for using a Matrix Diagram, which would apply to the situations you listed above?

☐ Useful tool for communicating responsibilities

☐ Useful to ensure everything is assigned

☐ Identifies who leads and who supports

☐ Allows team members to use respective strengths and skills

☐ Improves project planning and management

☐ Other: _______________________________

____

FORCE FIELD DIAGRAM

The Force Field Diagram is an analysis tool your team can use when:

- **You are trying to identify obstacles in reaching a goal**

- **You are trying to identify possible causes and solutions to a problem or an important opportunity**

- **Your team is stalled in achieving its goal**

The Force Field Diagram should be used by small groups (*five to seven*) of people working toward a common goal.

The following example shows how using a Force Field Diagram can help during focused improvement activities.

Lee, the Assistant Superintendent for School Policy, ...

was working with a team from the district office. They were given the task of identifying obstacles that stood in the way of the district's decision to hold year-round school. Year-round school was to be implemented by the next term. Lee had seen the Force Field Diagram in action and liked how the team members were able to quickly determine potential obstacles, as well as solutions, to the issue they were tackling....

Step 1: Prepare For The Force Field Diagram Session

At the start of your Force Field session:

➡ Create a flip chart or bring an overhead transparency of a Force Field Diagram *(see Diagram # 8)*.

➡ Provide a time limit to the session. Generally, setting aside 30 to 50 minutes is a good start.

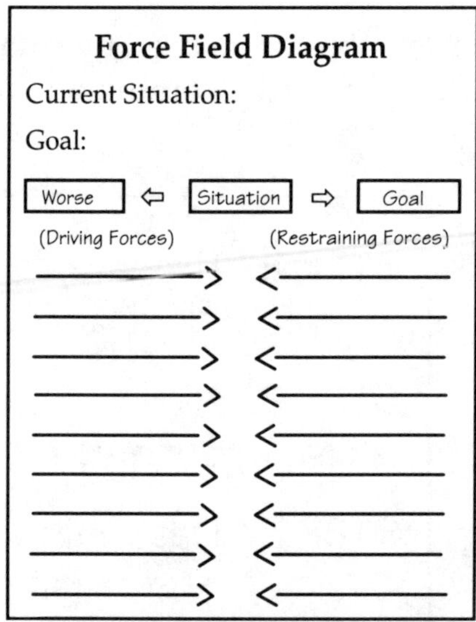

Diagram # 8 - Force Field Diagram

➡ Identify one or more Recorders. The job of the Recorder is to write down *(on a flip chart or overhead transparency)* the driving and restraining forces as they are called out.

➡ Use the ground rules of Brainstorming *(see Chapter Two)*.

Lee called the team together ...

for a 40-minute Force Field session covering the guidelines of how and why to use Force Field analysis. Lee asked Chris to record the team's ideas on a flip chart prepared for the session. Chris agreed, grabbed several markers, and the session began....

Step 2: Agree On The Current Situation

⟶ The current situation simply refers to what is happening now that you want to change or improve. This is always a current issue that needs to be resolved. Write the current situation on the Force Field Diagram.

⟶ If the team understands the current situation, chances are you have already clarified your goal. Just to be sure, validate with your team what the goal is. Come to agreement on the goal, and write it on the Force Field Diagram.

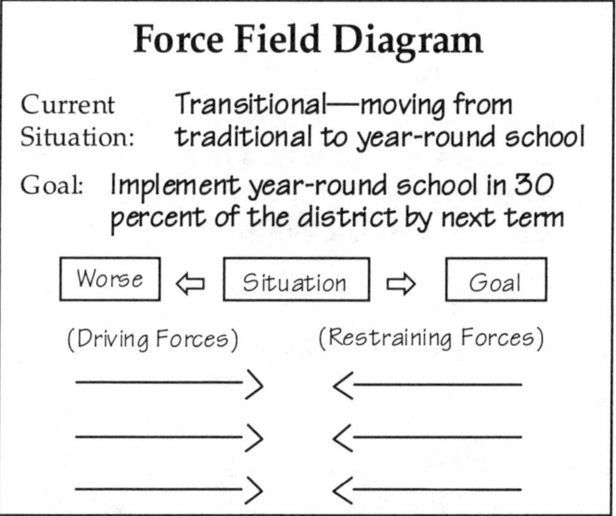

Diagram # 9 - Force Field Diagram with goal

Lee had no trouble convincing everyone …

that moving the district to year-round school would be a challenge. However, it was going to happen. The district had mandated it. The only question was how smoothly they could make the transition. After some discussion and information-sharing, they decided that the current situation could be described as a transitional one—moving from traditional to year-round school. Chris recorded this on the Force Field Diagram *(see Diagram # 9).*

With the situation defined, the team decided that a realistic goal would be to implement year-round school in 30 percent of the district by next term. Lee thought, *"This is great, it only took 10 minutes to get everyone to agree. The rest should be a piece of cake…."*

Step 3: Determine Driving And Restraining Forces

⟫➤ **Driving forces** are things *(actions, skills, equipment, procedures, culture, people, etc.)* that help move you toward your goal. **Restraining forces** are things that can keep you from reaching your goal.

⟫➤ As a group, ask the question, *"What things are 'driving' us toward our goal?"*

⟫➤ The Recorder should write down the responses on the left side of the Force Field Diagram *(see Diagram # 10).* Responses are written as they are called out, with space left between each response. Continue this until all driving forces have been recorded.

⟫➤ Then ask the question, *"What is 'restraining' us from achieving our goal?"*

⟫➤ The Recorder then writes the responses down on the right side of the Force Field Diagram *(see Diagram # 10).* Again, responses are written as they are called out, with space left between each response. Continue this until all restraining forces have been recorded.

As the team members started to call out ...

the driving and restraining forces, Chris busily recorded the ideas on the flip chart. Things were starting to get a little wild, so Lee asked everyone to slow down and offer one idea at a time. The team members were excited because they were actually identifying potential obstacles or restraining forces to reaching their goal....

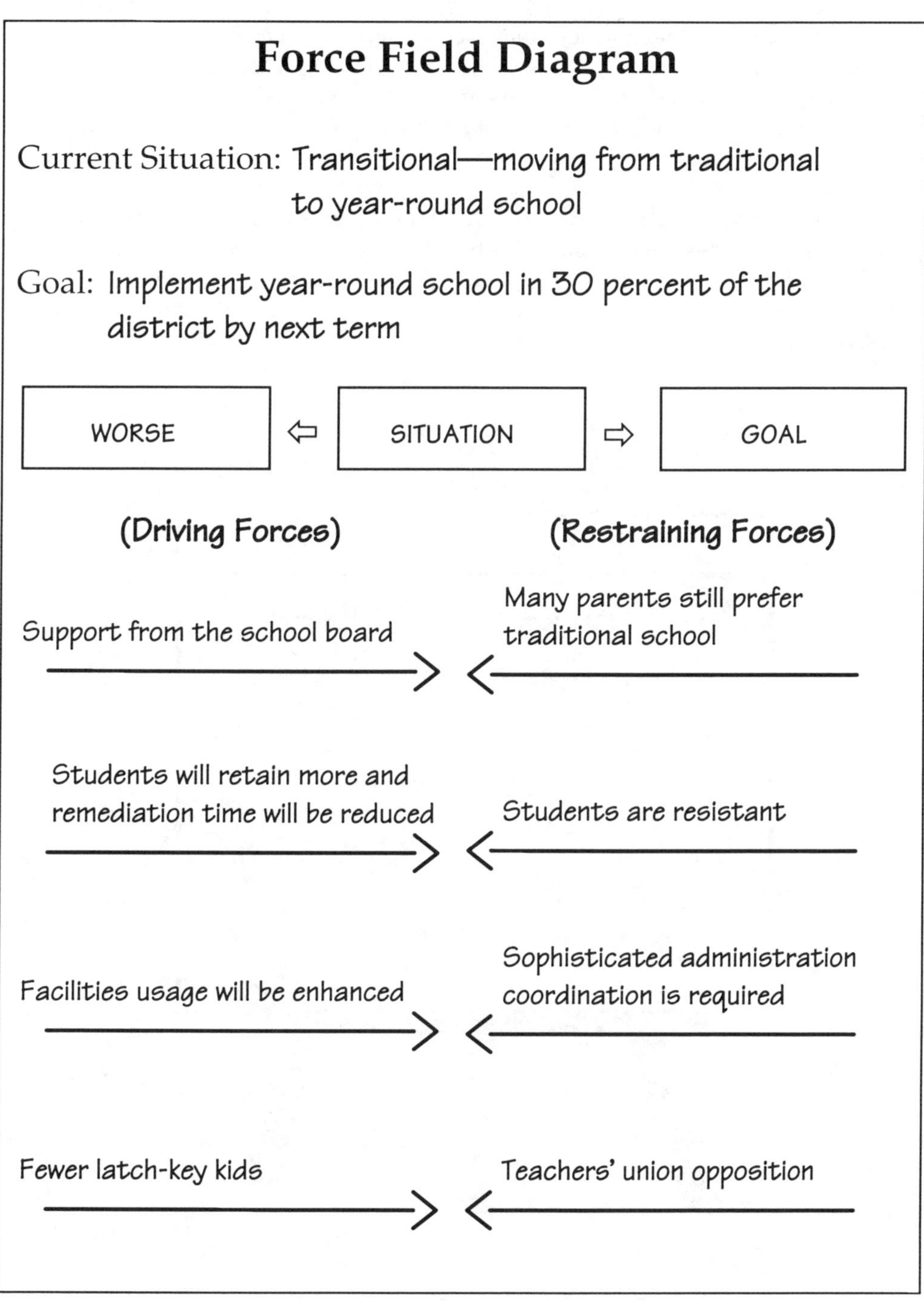

Diagram # 10 - Record driving and restraining forces

After 20 minutes, the team …

came up with 15 driving and restraining forces. Lee knew they may have missed some, but felt confident that they covered the major points. The team agreed the next step was to try to *"dig deeper"* for the causes of the restraining forces by asking why each one was happening *(see Diagram # 11).* This process took 18 minutes and produced several ideas on what was causing the various restraining forces.

The team assigned action items to several members, asking them to gather data verifying ideas on the major restraining forces. Lee thanked Chris and the rest of the team for their time. Lee felt confident the superintendent would respond well to their ideas about what might prevent a smooth transition to year-round school.

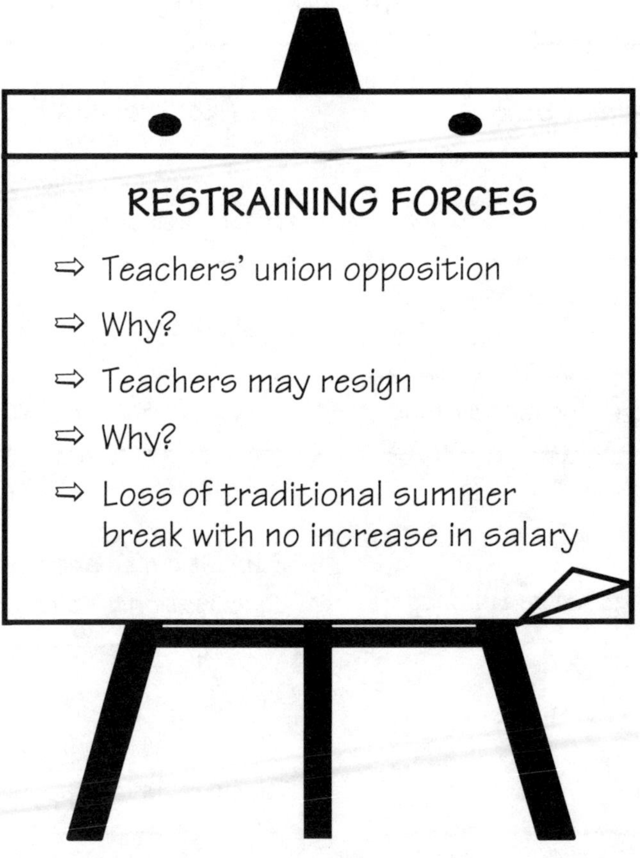

Diagram # 11 - Ask "Why?"

Decide On Next Steps

You know it's time to end the Force Field session when:

What to do next?

➠ Your team should prioritize the driving and restraining forces. Begin to eliminate the restraining forces and capitalize on the driving forces.

➠ Your team may sort the driving and restraining forces based on common themes *(see Affinity Diagram in Chapter Three)*.

➠ Your team should gather data to prove or disprove driving or restraining forces.

In summary, use the Force Field Diagram when:

☑ You are trying to identify the restraining forces in reaching a goal. *(By identifying the restraining forces, teams can determine what needs to be done to eliminate these restraints and concentrate on the driving forces.)*

☑ You are trying to identify possible causes and solutions to a problem or an improvement opportunity. *(On the Force Field Diagram, the driving forces can act as solutions, while the restraining forces can act as causes of the problem.)*

☑ Your team is stalled in achieving its goals. *(A large portion of completing a Force Field Diagram is Brainstorming possible restraining forces. The activity of identifying them can be helpful to a team that is stalled.)*

CHAPTER FIVE WORKSHEET:
FORCE FIELD DIAGRAM—IDEAS FOR USE

1. List the specific opportunities you have to use the Force Field Diagram.

____

____

____

____

____

2. What forces—driving *versus* restraining—do you think your team will be able to identify more of, and why?

☐ Driving Forces. Why?

____

____

____

☐ Restraining Forces. Why?

____

____

____

CAUSE AND EFFECT DIAGRAM

The Cause And Effect Diagram (*also known as the Fishbone Diagram*) is an analysis tool you can use to:

- **Categorize many potential causes of a problem or issue in an orderly way**

- **Analyze what is really happening in a process**

- **Teach teams and individuals about current or new processes and procedures**

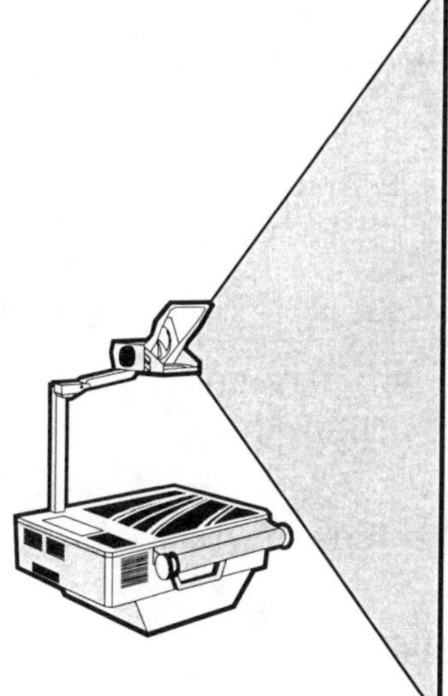

In the next example, an administrator faced with failing test scores uses the Cause And Effect Diagram to get to the *"root cause"* of a problem.

> ### *José, a test administrator at a local high school, …*
> was tired of taking criticism from teachers for students' failing test scores—as if he could do anything about it. *"What can I do?"* José asked himself. *"I administer the tests. If the teachers don't teach, it's not my problem."* José knew his principal didn't want any more excuses. Everyone wanted to see test scores improve.…

Step 1: Prepare For The Cause And Effect Session

Before you begin your Cause And Effect Analysis:

⇒ Create a flip chart or an overhead transparency, based on the example in Diagram # 12.

⇒ Provide a time limit for the session. Generally, 60 minutes is a reasonable amount of time.

⇒ Identify a Recorder. The job of the Recorder is to write down *(on a flip chart or overhead transparency)* the potential causes as they are called out.

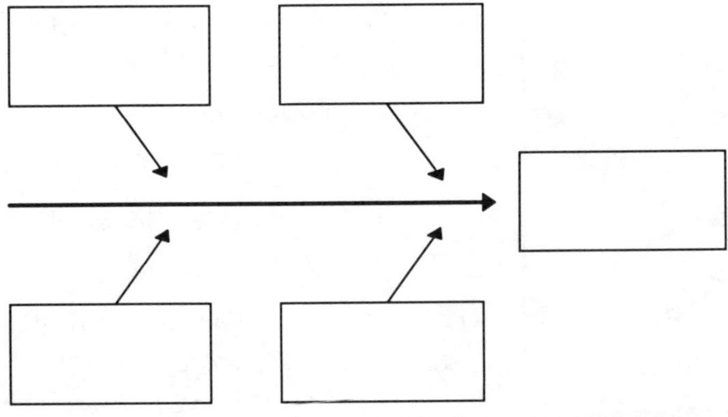

Diagram # 12 - Cause And Effect Diagram

Note: The Recorder does not necessarily decide which category the potential cause belongs in—that is a group decision.

José called together several department heads ...

for a 60-minute meeting to get to the bottom of the problem. He decided to try the Cause And Effect Diagram, because he had heard it was a good way to get to the root cause of problems. Prior to the meeting, José made a large Cause And Effect Diagram on two pieces of flip-chart paper and taped it to the wall of the conference room. He decided that for this first meeting he would be the Recorder....

Step 2: Identify The Effect

The effect refers to the issue *(problem or process condition)* you are trying to change. Write the effect in the box on the right side of the Cause And Effect Diagram.

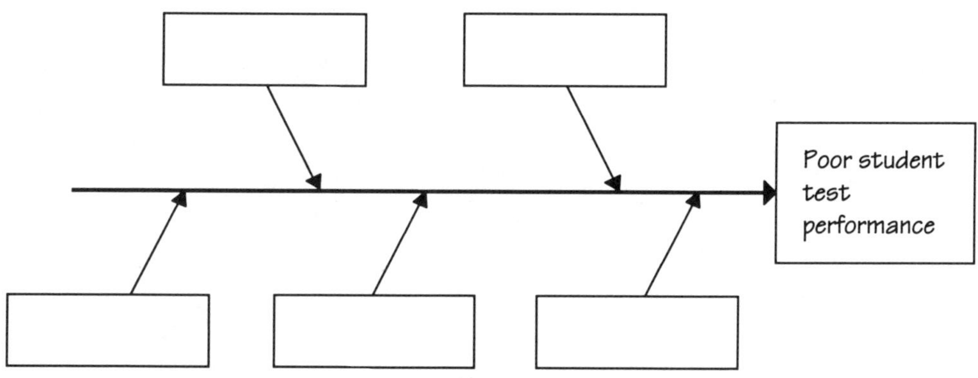

Diagram # 13 - Cause And Effect Diagram with problem identified

José began the meeting by ...

reminding all those present why they were there. *"This is everyone's problem. We all want to see our students perform better on the mandated tests,"* he said. *"Let's put our heads together and try to get to the bottom of this problem."* After that he wrote, *"Poor student test performance,"* in the box on the right side of the Cause And Effect Diagram *(see Diagram # 13)....*

Step 3: Identify The Major Cause Categories

➭ The diagonal lines that *"branch"* off the main horizontal line of the Cause And Effect Diagram are called major cause categories. You can use major cause categories to organize the causes in a way that makes the most sense for your specific situation.

You can summarize causes under categories such as:

➭ Methods, Machines, Materials, People *(the 3 M's and a P)*

➭ Places, Procedures, People, Policies *(the 4 P's)*

➭ Surroundings, Suppliers, Systems, Skills *(the 4 S's)*

Remember, these categories are only suggestions; you may use any category that helps you organize your ideas.

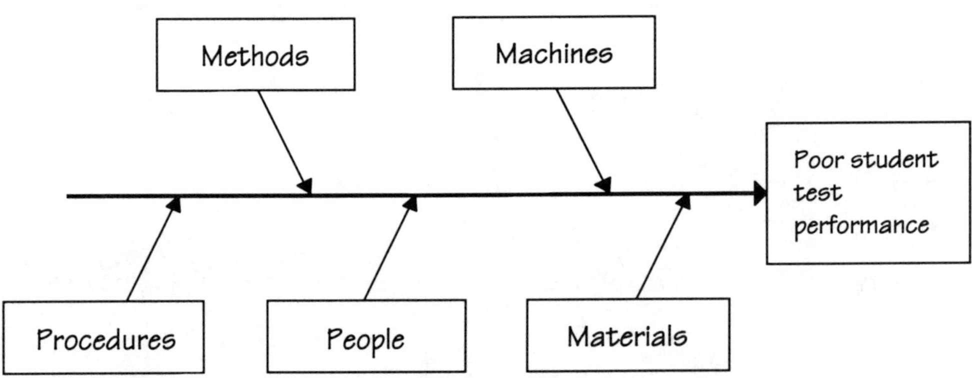

Diagram # 14 - Cause And Effect Diagram with cause categories

José wrote the 3 M's and a P ...

at the end of each of the diagonal lines. The team decided that another major cause category was needed, so José added one labeled *"Procedures"* *(see Diagram # 14)....*

Step 4: Brainstorm Potential Causes Of The Problem

➡ Follow the steps for Brainstorming listed in Chapter Two.

➡ As possible causes are called out, decide as a group where to place them on the Cause And Effect Diagram *(i.e., decide under which major cause category they should be placed)*.

➡ It's acceptable to list a possible cause under more than one major cause category *(e.g., receiving late data could go under both People and Procedures)*.

➡ Try to list many possible causes on the Cause And Effect Diagram at this point.

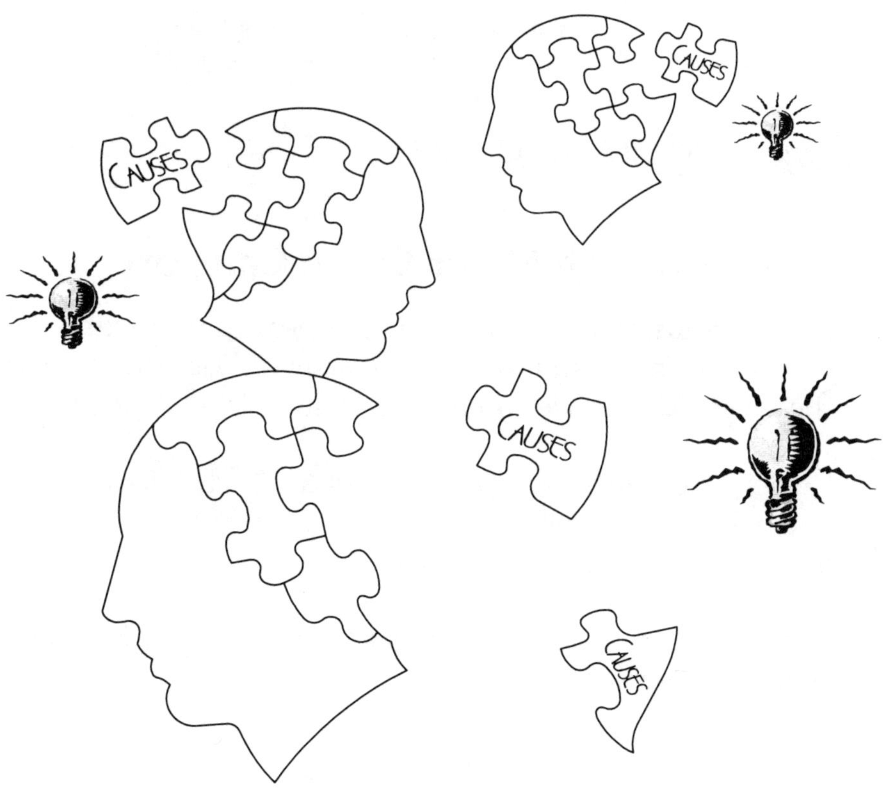

José had led Brainstorming sessions before, ...

so he was familiar with the process. As the team called out each possible cause, he asked which cause category to list it under *(see Diagram # 15)*. Some causes were easy, while others were more difficult to pigeonhole and ended up in two or more categories. This process continued for 25 minutes....

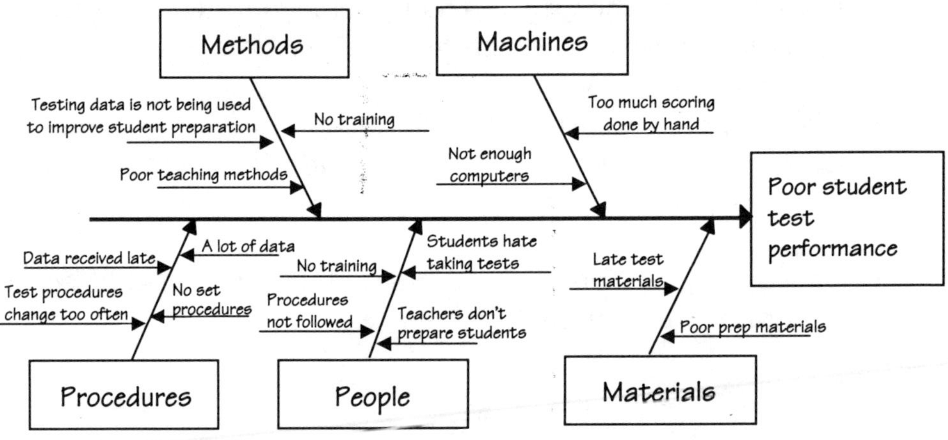

Diagram # 15 - Cause And Effect Diagram with potential causes

Step 5: Review Each Major Cause Category

⟫ At this point, look for causes that appear in more than one category. This is an indication of a *"most likely cause."* Circle the most likely causes on the diagram. *(See Diagram # 16.)*

⟫ Review the causes that you've circled *(the most likely causes)* and ask, *"Why is this a cause?"* Asking *"why?"* will help you get to the root cause of the problem.

⟫ Record the answers to your *"why?"* questions on a separate sheet of flip-chart paper.

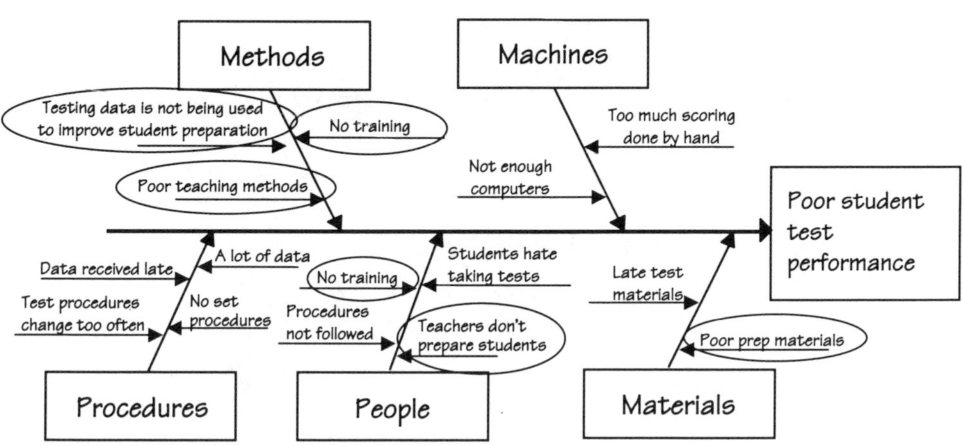

Diagram # 16 - Focus on root causes

When the team realized ...

that a few of the causes appeared repeatedly *(e.g., student preparation, teaching methods, and lack of training)*, José began asking a series of *"why"* questions *(e.g., "Why aren't students prepared? Why are our teaching methods inadequate? Why is there little or no training?, etc.)*.

José then asked *"why?"* regarding the answers of the first questions. In doing this, the team sifted through the symptoms to get to the true root cause(s) of the problem. They felt a little uncomfortable with this process at first *(it felt a bit like an interrogation)*, but soon realized they were actually getting to the root cause(s) *(see Diagram # 17)....*

Step 6: Reach An Agreement On Most Probable Cause(s)

➠ After you narrow down the most likely causes, choose from that group those you feel are the most probable causes.

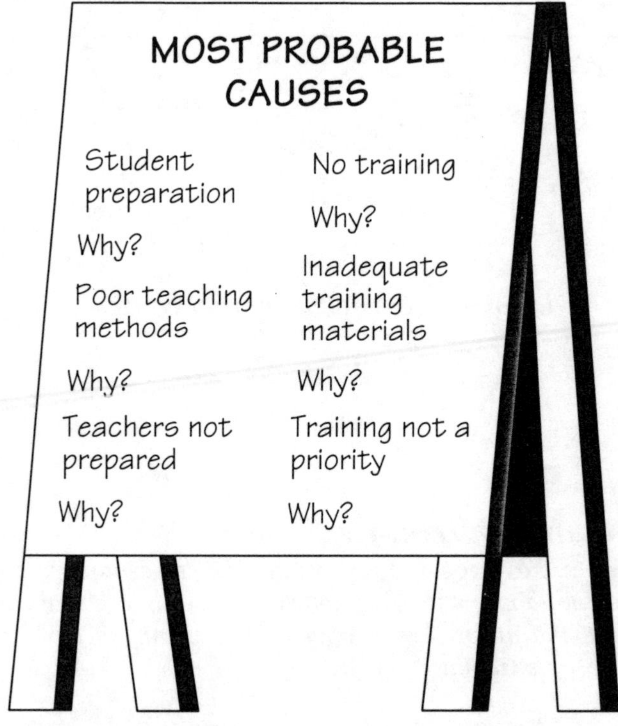

Diagram # 17 - Top two causes

After about 50 minutes, ...

the team had identified what they thought were the top two most probable causes of poor student test performance. The next step was to develop some type of measurement to determine whether they were right.

Kim volunteered to develop a survey that would measure teacher priorities and percent of time allocated to subject areas. Meanwhile, Marie took on the task of determining if training materials were available. José thanked all present for their time and effort and asked the team to meet at the same time the following week.

Decide On Next Steps

You know it's time to end the Cause And Effect session when:

In summary, use the Cause And Effect Diagram when:

☑ You want to categorize many potential causes of a problem or issue in an easy-to-understand, orderly way. *(By breaking a process down into a number of process-related categories—such as: people, materials, machinery, procedures, policies, etc.—your team is able to better identify the possible causes of a problem.)*

☑ You want to analyze what is really happening in a process. *(i.e., By breaking a process down into a number of process-related categories, the Cause And Effect Diagram can provide a picture of the actual process condition.)*

☑ You are teaching teams and individuals about new processes and procedures. *(i.e., You can use the Cause And Effect Diagram to train and/or explain how a process works.)*

CHAPTER SIX WORKSHEET:
CAUSE AND EFFECT DIAGRAM—IDEAS FOR USE

1. List the specific opportunities you have to use the Cause And Effect Diagram.

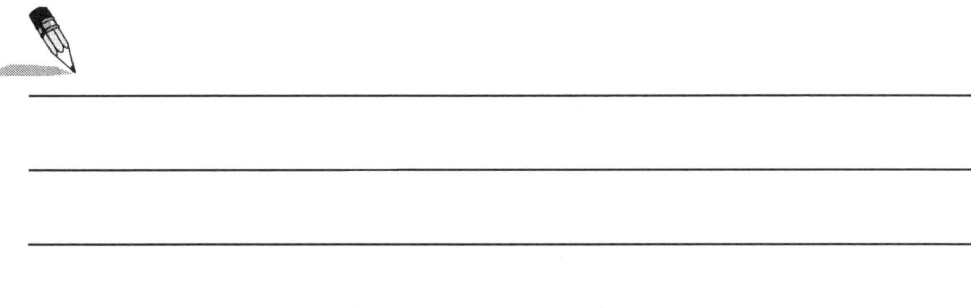

2. Identify and list major *cause categories* that might be appropriate for one of the situations you noted above.

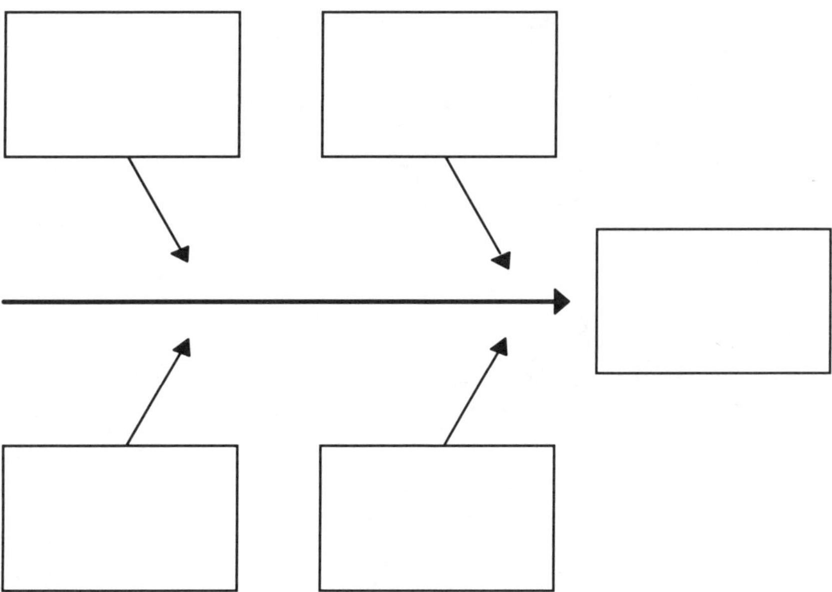

CRITERIA RATING FORM

The Criteria Rating Form is an interpretation tool you can use to select ideas and solutions from among several alternatives.

Use the Criteria Rating Form when:

- ☞ **You have to select among several alternatives**

- ☞ **You want to make a decision objectively**

- ☞ **You want your group to agree on a decision**

In the following example, a team is having trouble making a decision about the brand of computers to purchase for three new computer labs.

Janet was the leader of a team ...

chosen to recommend computers to go in the new computer labs. She was feeling extreme pressure. One of the *"more vocal"* college professors was pushing for Byna 686's, the slightly lower cost alternative. A recent consumer magazine recommended Quartel 686. To add more confusion to the mix, most team members favored the MacGregor 6. It was already Tuesday afternoon, and Janet had to have the team's recommendations on the dean's desk by Friday morning at 9:00 am!

Step 1: Start The Session And List The Alternatives Available

At the start of your Criteria Rating session:

➠ Have a Criteria Rating Form prepared on a flip chart or an overhead transparency *(see Diagram # 18)*.

➠ Provide a time limit for the session. Generally, 45 to 60 minutes is sufficient.

➠ Select a Recorder.

➠ List the available alternatives along the top of the Criteria Rating Form.

Note: You may have to generate alternatives by Brainstorming.

> ## *First thing Wednesday morning, …*
> Janet called the team members into a conference room. All of them knew that this was the moment of truth. They *had* to reach an agreement on which computers to purchase. Janet suggested they use the Criteria Rating process to help them make the decision.…

CRITERIA RATING FORM

Criteria	Weight	ALTERNATIVES		
		Byna 686	Quartel 686	MacGregor 6
Total				
Summary				

Diagram # 18 - The Criteria Rating Form

Step 2: Brainstorm Decision Criteria

You will be judging the *"alternatives"* against what you feel are the most important qualities each one should have. These qualities are called decision criteria. We use decision criteria all the time.

For example, when we are choosing a car to buy, we look at criteria such as cost, length of warranty, availability of service, etc. If more than one person is making the decision, it's advantageous to agree on the decision criteria. Then the decision-making process runs more smoothly.

Common criteria include:

Selection Criteria

➪ Ease of implementation

➪ Lowest cost

➪ Ability to meet stakeholder requirements

➪ Resource availability

➪ Lowest risk

➪ Fastest to implement

➪ Long-term workability

Remember, the criteria may change for each project you're working on.

➠ Your group should determine the criteria through Brainstorming *(see Chapter Two for guidelines on Brainstorming)*, and then list reduction.

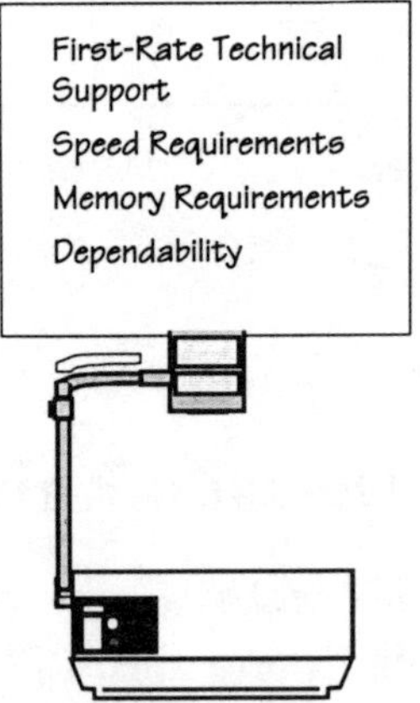

After a heated (but friendly) discussion, ...

the team agreed on the criteria for judging each alternative. Janet turned on the overhead projector and wrote out the reduced list of selection criteria *(see Diagram # 19)*. The team felt that the most important features of the new computers should include: first-rate technical support; functionality that meets speed and memory requirements; and dependability *(cost became a non-issue since all the computer alternatives were in the same price range)*....

Step 3: Determine The Relative Importance Of Each Criterion

))) Give each of the criterion a weight *(that represents its relative importance)*.

))) To determine the weight of each criterion, ask, *"How important is each of the criterion in relationship to the others?"*

))) Remember, the total of the assigned weights for all criteria must equal 100 percent.

))) The effectiveness of the Criteria Rating process is heavily dependent upon the weighting of the criteria. Ensure integrity in weighting decisions by getting input from all team members. For unbiased input, ask each individual team member to assign weights to the criteria. Average the individual weights assigned by each team member, and then determine the final weight.

		ALTERNATIVES		
Criteria	**Weight**	Byna 686	Quartel 686	MacGregor 6
Technical Support	40%			
Speed	20%			
Memory	20%			
Dependability	20%			
Total	100%			
Summary				

Diagram # 19 - The Criteria Rating Form with weights

Janet asked the team to review the criteria ...

and decide how important each one was in relation to the others. She then asked them to assign each criterion a percentage that represented its priority, *(e.g., 10 percent would be a low priority, 70 percent would equal a high priority)*, reminding everyone that the total of all the ratings must equal 100 percent. Janet gave the team five minutes to rate the list of criteria, while she filled in a Criteria Rating Form on the flip chart....

Step 4: Establish A Rating Scale; Rate The Alternatives

Rating Scale: **10** = high, **1** = low

		ALTERNATIVES		
Criteria	**Weight**	Byna 686	Quartel 686	MacGregor 6
Technical Support	40%	8	5	3
Speed	20%	6	8	7
Memory	20%	6	4	4
Dependability	20%	6	7	7
Total	100%			
Summary				

Diagram # 20 - The Criteria Rating Form with weights and ratings

➠ Your team must use a consistent rating scale to compare the various alternatives against each criterion. Any scale will work as long as you use the same scale for all alternatives and criteria. An easy scale to use is 1 to 10, with 10 being high and 1 being low.

➠ Each alternative should be rated against each criterion using the established rating scale. It is possible that the rating can only be determined after an investigation (*e.g., you may have to verify which alternative costs less*).

The team was ready to rate ...

each of the alternatives against each criterion (*see Diagram # 20*). First, they worked individually. Then, the team shared responses. Not surprisingly—since all the team members had reviewed the research notes—the ratings were close, and consensus was quickly reached. The Byna 686 rated highest in technical support and memory, while both the Quartel 686 and the MacGregor 6 rated higher in speed and dependability....

Step 5: Calculate The Final Score

➧ Multiply the weight *(established in Step 3)* by the rating for each alternative *(established in Step 4)*.

➧ Write this figure in parentheses in the appropriate boxes on the Criteria Rating Form.

➧ Add the numbers in parentheses for each alternative and write the totals in the appropriate boxes.

➧ Write any summary comments in the appropriate boxes.

To come up with a score, ...

Janet recorded each of the ratings directly on the Criteria Rating flip chart and asked Michael *(the only team member with a calculator)* to multiply each of the ratings by the weight. As Michael finished multiplying, Janet recorded the answers *(in parentheses)* on the flip chart. Michael then added each of the numbers in parentheses, and Janet wrote
the final totals in the appropriate boxes on the bottom of the flip chart
(see Diagram # 21)....

		ALTERNATIVES		
Criteria	**Weight**	Byna 686	Quartel 686	MacGregor 6
Technical Support	40%	8 x .4 (3.2)	5 x .4 (2.0)	3 x .4 (1.2)
Speed	20%	6 x .2 (1.2)	8 x .2 (1.6)	7 x .2 (1.4)
Memory	20%	6 x .2 (1.2)	4 x .2 (.8)	4 x .2 (.8)
Dependability	20%	6 x .2 (1.2)	7 x .2 (1.4)	7 x .2 (1.4)
Total	100%	6.8	5.8	4.8
Summary				

Diagram # 21 - The Criteria Rating Form with totals

Step 6: Select The Best Alternative

⟩⟩➡ Select the alternative that has the highest total score.

⟩⟩➡ This alternative may or may not be the one ultimately chosen. The alternative with the highest score should be the best. If the team members don't agree, they should review the weighting of the criteria and the ratings and make necessary changes.

> **Note:** Use the summary boxes to record any notes about the alternatives.

⟩⟩➡ If necessary, repeat the process.

		ALTERNATIVES		
Criteria	**Weight**	Byna 686	Quartel 686	MacGregor 6
Technical Support	40%	8 x .4 (3.2)	5 x .4 (2.0)	3 x .4 (1.2)
Speed	20%	6 x .2 (1.2)	8 x .2 (1.6)	7 x 2 (1.4)
Memory	20%	6 x .2 (1.2)	4 x .2 (.8)	4 x .2 (.8)
Dependability	20%	6 x .2 (1.2)	7 x .2 (1.4)	7 x .2 (1.4)
Total	100%	(6.8)	5.8	4.8
Summary		✓		

Diagram # 22 - Select the best alternative

Based on the weighting of the criteria ...

and the rating of each of the alternatives, the Byna 686 had the highest total (*see Diagram # 22*). The Quartel and the MacGregor finished second and third respectively. It was clear the Byna won because it had the highest technical support rating and memory, and it wasn't far behind the other models in speed, and dependability. Although not everyone originally agreed on the Byna, it was hard to argue with its superiority now. After all, everyone had an equal voice in the weighting and rating process. The team had reached a true consensus....

Decide On Next Steps

You know it's time to stop the Criteria Rating session when:

Since the technical support issue was so important ...

the team decided to investigate further. They needed clarification from Byna on three points: would a Byna 686 purchase include 24-hour telephone support?; on-site repair within one working day?; and if a computer had to be repaired off-site, what was their turn-around time?

Denise volunteered to call Byna and verify the team's findings. She committed to having an answer by the following day. Janet and the team were happy with the results of the session. They felt confident that they could make a recommendation to the dean by Friday morning.

In summary, use the Criteria Rating Form when:

☑ You have to select between several alternatives. *(The Criteria Rating method will help your decision-making process by providing a step-by-step procedure.)*

☑ You want to include more objectivity into a decision-making process. *(The Criteria Rating method takes subjectivity out of the decision-making process by assigning weights and rankings to each potential solution.)*

☑ You want a consensus-building tool that will help your team reach a decision. *(The Criteria Rating method helps to build consensus by taking opinion out of the decision-making process.)*

CHAPTER SEVEN WORKSHEET:
THE CRITERIA RATING FORM—IDEAS FOR USE

1. List some specific opportunities you have to use the Criteria Rating Form.

____

____

____

2. List the criteria you might use in an upcoming situation. What weights would you assign to them?

- ___________________________ ________ %
- ___________________________ ________ %
- ___________________________ ________ %
- ___________________________ ________ %
- ___________________________ ________ %
- ___________________________ ________ %

100%

3. How might your choice or weighting of criteria differ if you were working on a short-term instead of a long-term issue or problem?

____

____

____

____

CHECK SHEET

Use a Check Sheet as a data-gathering and interpretation tool when
you want to:

   ☞ **Distinguish between opinion and fact**

   ☞ **Gather data about how often a problem is occurring**

   ☞ **Gather data about the type of problem occurring**

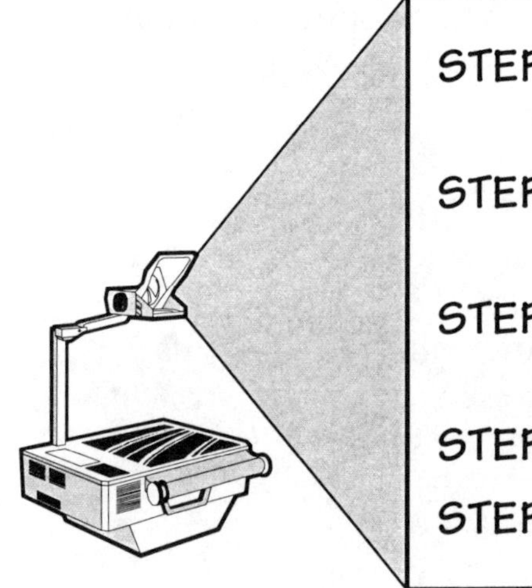

The following example shows how a Check Sheet can be used to
distinguish between opinion and fact.

Lori was concerned ...

her ninth grade English Composition classes were not performing up to expectations. She didn't expect them to win a Pulitzer, but she knew they could do a lot better. In addition, as the department chair, Lori was getting calls from the administration.

Principal Smith had gotten wind of district complaints because of poor test scores and called Lori. *"It's all about fundamentals,"* the Principal said, *"It's obvious to me that the reason these kids aren't performing is because they didn't learn what they were supposed to learn in middle school."* (Principal Smith was always a great one for pointing out the obvious.) The Principal continued, *"What happened to spelling bees and vocabulary drills?"*....

Step 1: Clarify Your Measurement Objectives

A good place to start when collecting data (*whether using a Check Sheet or not)* is to go through a process of asking some questions. Questions you should ask include:

➠ What is the problem?

➠ Why should data be collected?

➠ Who will use the information being collected and what information do they really need to see (*e.g., by department, by day, by month, by student, by class, by subject area, etc.*)?

➠ Who will collect the data?

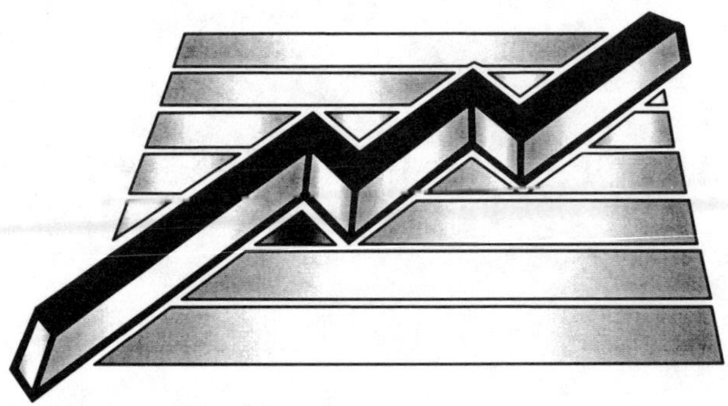

Lori agreed that there was a problem ...

with student performance in the English composition classes. However, the specific questions were *where* was the deficiency and *how* could the problem be corrected.

What was clear was that her principal was getting heat from parents and the district office. It was beginning to feel uncomfortably warm in her direction. The first thing she needed to do was to collect student performance data. She wanted to target her instruction efforts where they would be of greatest benefit....

Lori was able to get a tally of common composition errors by looking at student papers from the last quarter. She asked the English teachers to keep a monthly Check Sheet of writing errors. Since she wanted to measure various types of errors over a period of time and get a *"snapshot"* of the situation, she decided to make a Check Sheet of the complaint data from the previous two months....

Step 2: Identify What You Are Measuring

⟫ Begin by giving your Check Sheet a title. The title should tell readers what they are looking at (*e.g., parent complaints, discipline problems, tardiness, first quarter grades, unexcused absences, etc.*).

⟫ Next, write only the specific things you are going to measure down the left side of the Check Sheet. For example, if you are measuring parent complaints, possible categories could include late busses, rude driver, etc.

STUDENT ERRORS ON ENGLISH COMPOSITION PAPERS

Error Category							
Spelling							
Sentence Structure							
Story Development							
Use of Vocabulary							
Total							

Diagram # 23 - Check Sheet with complaint types

Lori spent about two hours ...

sifting through data and papers from the previous quarter. After reading through the data, she decided that errors fell into four major categories. She named the Check Sheet *"Student Errors On English Composition Papers"* and started filling it in....

Step 3: Determine The Time Or Place Being Measured

⟹ Decide whether you want to collect information based on time *(e.g., how many things happen per hour or day)* or by place, or both *(e.g., how many things happen in Department A each day, number of times driver X was late, accidents by location or by month, etc.).*

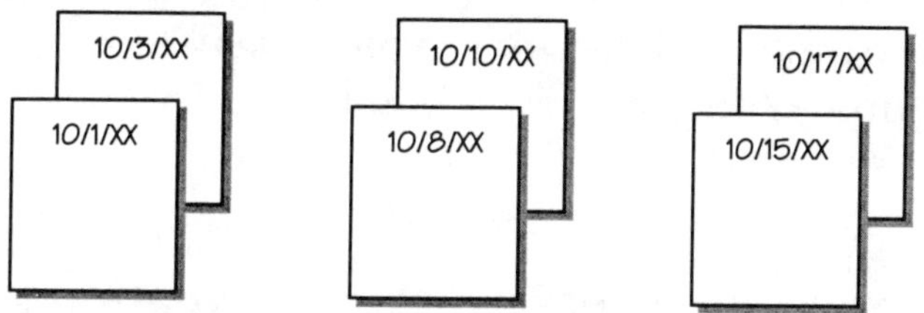

Since students turned in two papers ...

per week *(on Wednesdays and Fridays)*, Lori set up her sheet with six columns to cover a three-week period *(see diagram # 24)*. She expected that some trends might surface. For example, would she see an increase in errors on Friday when students were more focused on the weekend and less on writing? Lori distributed a Check Sheet to each English teacher....

STUDENT ERRORS ON ENGLISH COMPOSITION PAPERS DURING A THREE-WEEK PERIOD

Error Category	Wed. 10/1/XX	Fri. 10/3/XX	Wed. 10/8/XX	Fri. 10/10/XX	Wed. 10/15/XX	Fri. 10/17/XX	Total
Spelling							
Sentence Structure							
Story Development							
Use of Vocabulary							
Total							

Diagram # 24 - Blank student English composition errors Check Sheet

Step 4: Collect The Data

➠ Begin collecting data for the items you are measuring.

Record each occurrence directly on the Check Sheet as it happens.

Since accuracy is essential when collecting data *(after all, you will be making decisions based on this data)*, don't wait until the end of the day or when you are on a break to record information. You may forget it in the meantime.

For three weeks, Lori entered the information ...

onto the Check Sheet. She was surprised by the results. It looked as if most of the errors were related to story development. At the end of three weeks, she received current Check Sheets from the other English teachers, and the results were similar *(see diagram # 25)*. She was beginning to think that maybe she and Principal Smith had indeed jumped—*no, soared*—to conclusions about causes....

STUDENT ERRORS ON ENGLISH COMPOSITION PAPERS DURING A THREE-WEEK PERIOD

Error Category	Wed. 10/1/XX	Fri. 10/3/XX	Wed. 10/8/XX	Fri. 10/10/XX	Wed. 10/15/XX	Fri. 10/17/XX	Total
Spelling	I	I	II	I	I	II	
Sentence Structure	II	I	III	I			
Story Development	IIII	卌	IIII	III	卌	III	
Use of Vocabulary	III	I	II	III	II		
Total							

Diagram # 25 - Student English composition errors during a three-week period

Step 5: Total The Data

➧ Total the number of occurrences for each category being measured (*e.g., how many times were students late this week, how many data entry errors were made at district office XYZ today, etc.*).

STUDENT ERRORS ON ENGLISH COMPOSITION PAPERS DURING A THREE-WEEK PERIOD

Error Category	Wed. 10/1/XX	Fri. 10/3/XX	Wed. 10/8/XX	Fri. 10/10/XX	Wed. 10/15/XX	Fri. 10/17/XX	Total
Spelling	I	I	I I	I	I	I I	8
Sentence Structure	I I	I	I I I	I			7
Story Development	I I I I	++++	I I I I	I I I	++++	I I I	24
Use of Vocabulary	I I I	I	I I	I I I	I I		11
Total	10	8	11	8	8	5	

Diagram # 26 - Completed student English composition errors Check Sheet

After recording all the information ...

on the Check Sheet, Lori added up the tally marks for each type of error for each day and wrote them in the appropriate boxes (*see Diagram # 26*)....

Decide On Next Steps

➧ Decide on an appropriate interpretation method.

➧ Make decisions based on fact (*not just opinion*) about what you are measuring. Since you have data, you can decide how to begin making needed improvements.

➧ Continue to collect data to verify your original findings and to evaluate any changes (*improvements*) you make.

After reviewing the weekly data ...

for a six-week period, Lori felt confident that story development accounted for the majority of student composition errors.

Her meeting with Principal Smith was scheduled for the next day, and she was going to be armed with the Check Sheets from the last six weeks. *"Even Principal Smith,"* she thought, *"can't argue with data."* Lori and the other English teachers knew that if changes were going to be made in the English curriculum, more information would be needed—so they continued to collect the weekly data on student compositions.

The process also held an added benefit of promoting team camaraderie in the English department. The team was on its way to success!

In summary, use the Check Sheet when you want to ...

☑ Distinguish between opinion and fact. *(We often think we know which problem, or underlying cause is most important. The Check Sheet helps to prove or disprove those opinions.)*

☑ Gather data about how often a problem is occurring. *(The main purpose of the Check Sheet is to help tabulate the number of occurrences of a given problem or cause.)*

☑ Gather data about the type of problem that is occurring. *(Check Sheets help you break down data into different categories such as causes, problems, etc.)*

CHAPTER EIGHT WORKSHEET:
CHECK SHEETS—IDEAS FOR USE

1. List the specific opportunities you have to use Check Sheets.

2. Of the situations you listed above, which one represents a pressing issue that needs to be taken care of soon? Why?

3. What type of data might you collect with the Check Sheet for this *"pressing"* situation?

CHAPTER NINE

SUMMARY

Consider your quality-improvement effort to be a *"construction project,"* such as building a house. You can assemble enthusiastic and able professionals, purchase the best building supplies available, even contract a renowned architect to design your house; but, if you don't have the right tools for the job, all your effort is wasted.

This analogy is appropriate for your own construction job— improving the quality of your school. You need the right tools— Brainstorming, the Affinity Diagram, the Force Field Diagram, the Matrix Diagram, the Cause And Effect Diagram, the Criteria Rating Form, and the Check Sheet—and you need to know how to use them correctly. This knowledge is essential to *"building"* your quality-improvement effort.

For any tool to be effective, you need to know how and when to apply it. Each tool presented in this guidebook is used in a different situation. For example, Brainstorming, the Affinity Diagram, and the Matrix Diagram are planning tools. The Force Field Diagram and the Cause And Effect Diagram are both analysis tools. The Criteria Rating Form is a planning tool, and the Check Sheet is an analysis tool. Both are also interpretation tools. See the Selection Matrix in Chapter One for a quick reference of the uses of all the tools in this guidebook and *Continuous Improvement Tools In Education, Volume 2.* Just as a hammer, a screwdriver, and a saw are used for different jobs, quality tools all have different primary functions as well.

We are all in the position to improve our jobs. The smallest of individual efforts can *(and often does)* add up to large organizational improvements. The examples used in this guidebook show how teams and individuals can use the tools *(as carpenters or cabinetmakers use the tools of their trade)* to *"build"* real improvements into their immediate jobs. By using these tools, you too can make a difference by building quality into education.

REPRODUCIBLE FORMS
AND WORKSHEETS

The pages in the Appendix are provided for you to photocopy and use appropriately.

MATRIX DIAGRAM WORKSHEET

Address the following questions when preparing to use a Matrix Diagram.

1. Determine the level at which you are defining the tasks. *(For each task, there may be subtasks, which may in turn have additional subtasks.)*

____

____

____

2. Define the specific outcome(s) of your project *(e.g., the specific, tangible, and intangible outcomes such as a report, a presentation, equipment installation, etc.).*

____

____

____

3. List all the tasks that you need to complete to achieve your desired outcome(s).

____

____

____

4. Do all the group members agree on the criteria for matching the tasks with the appropriate people *(e.g., time, expertise, learning opportunities, etc.)*? List any disagreements.

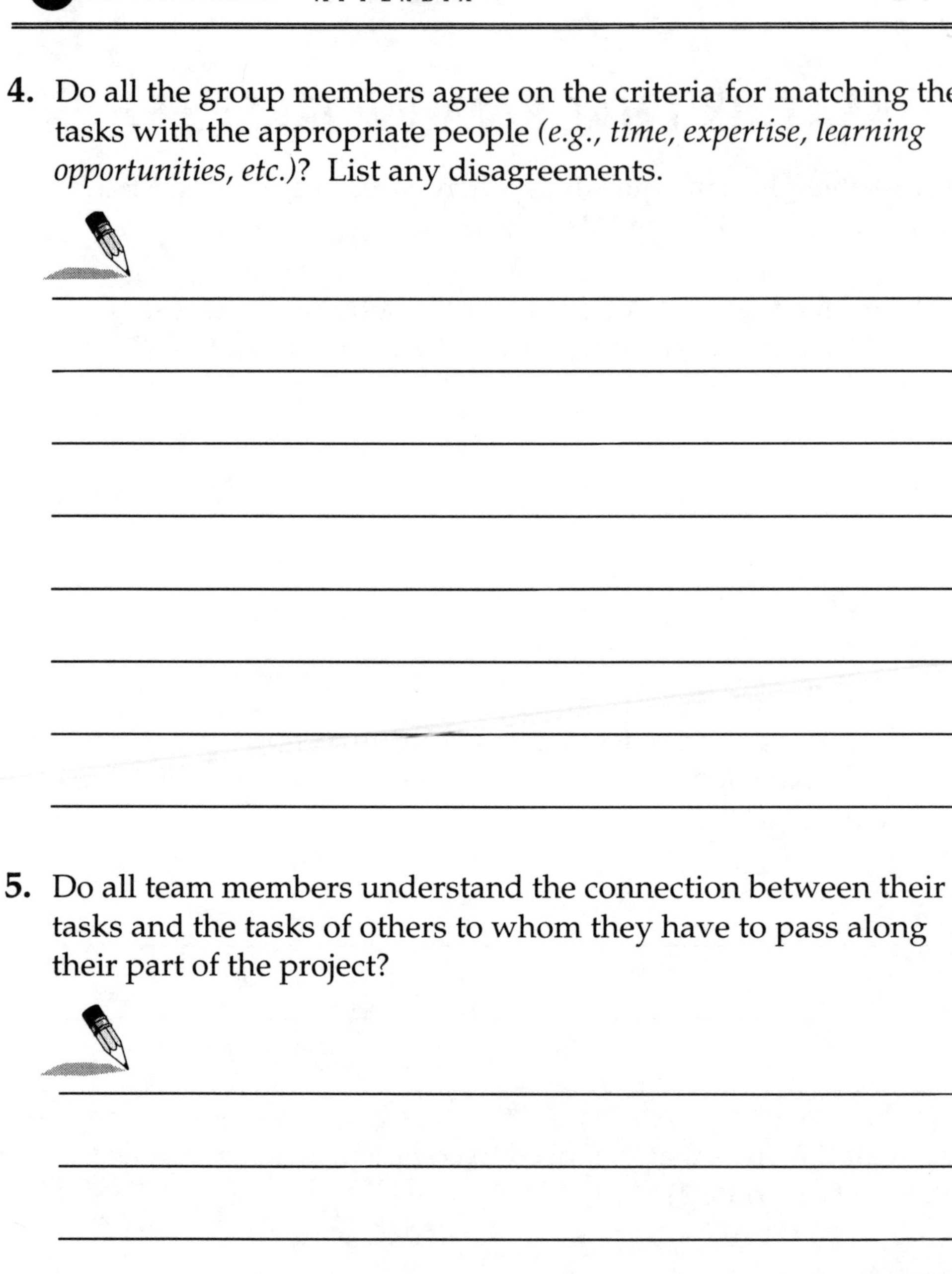

5. Do all team members understand the connection between their tasks and the tasks of others to whom they have to pass along their part of the project?

MATRIX DIAGRAM

RESPONSIBILITY / TASK									

FORCE FIELD DIAGRAM WORKSHEET

Address the following questions when preparing to use a Force
Field Diagram.

1. Describe the current situation. Is this definition agreed to by all
involved?

---

2. List the data supporting this definition of the current situation.

---

3. Describe the goal. Is there agreement on it?

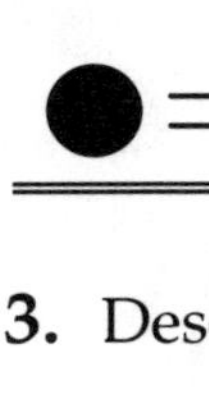

____

____

____

____

____

____

____

4. Who must be included to help determine actual *driving* and *restraining* forces?

____

____

____

____

____

____

FORCE FIELD DIAGRAM

Current Situation:

Goal:

| Worse | ⇐ | Situation | ⇒ | Goal |

(Driving Forces)   (Restraining Forces)

CAUSE AND EFFECT DIAGRAM WORKSHEET

Address the following questions when preparing to use the Cause And Effect Diagram:

1. Describe the issue or effect of the problem. Has it been clearly defined and agreed to?

____

____

____

____

2. List the major cause categories you will use.

____

____

____

____

3. Describe the process you will use to narrow down the list of possible causes your group brainstorms.

____

____

____

4. How will you get to the true root cause of the shorter list of probable causes that your group will develop?

---

5. Is your group going to be prepared to take on assignments to gather data or handle follow-up tasks? How will this be done?

CAUSE AND EFFECT DIAGRAM

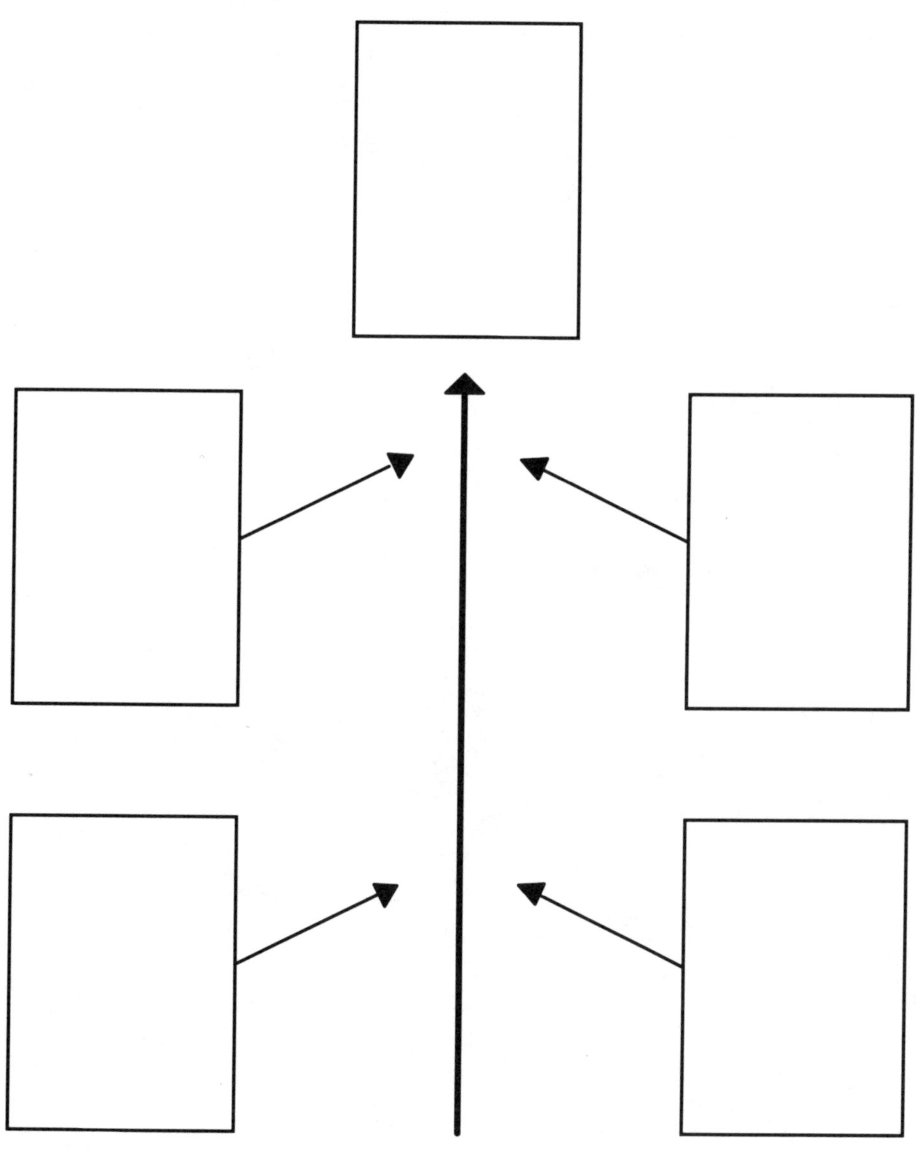

CRITERIA RATING FORM WORKSHEET

Address the following questions when preparing to use the Criteria Rating Form:

1. Have you narrowed down your list of alternatives to a manageable number—approximately six or less? Or, if necessary, have you agreed on a process* to help you arrive at a relatively short list? Write down your short list.

____

____

____

____

2. Do you have the right criteria to fit the specific situation you are working with? List your criteria.

____

____

____

____

____

* *Team Decision-Making Techniques In Education* is another Practical Guidebook with great tools to help your team make decisions and narrow alternatives, criteria, etc., along the way.

3. Has everyone involved come to a consensus on the weighting of the criteria? If not, why?

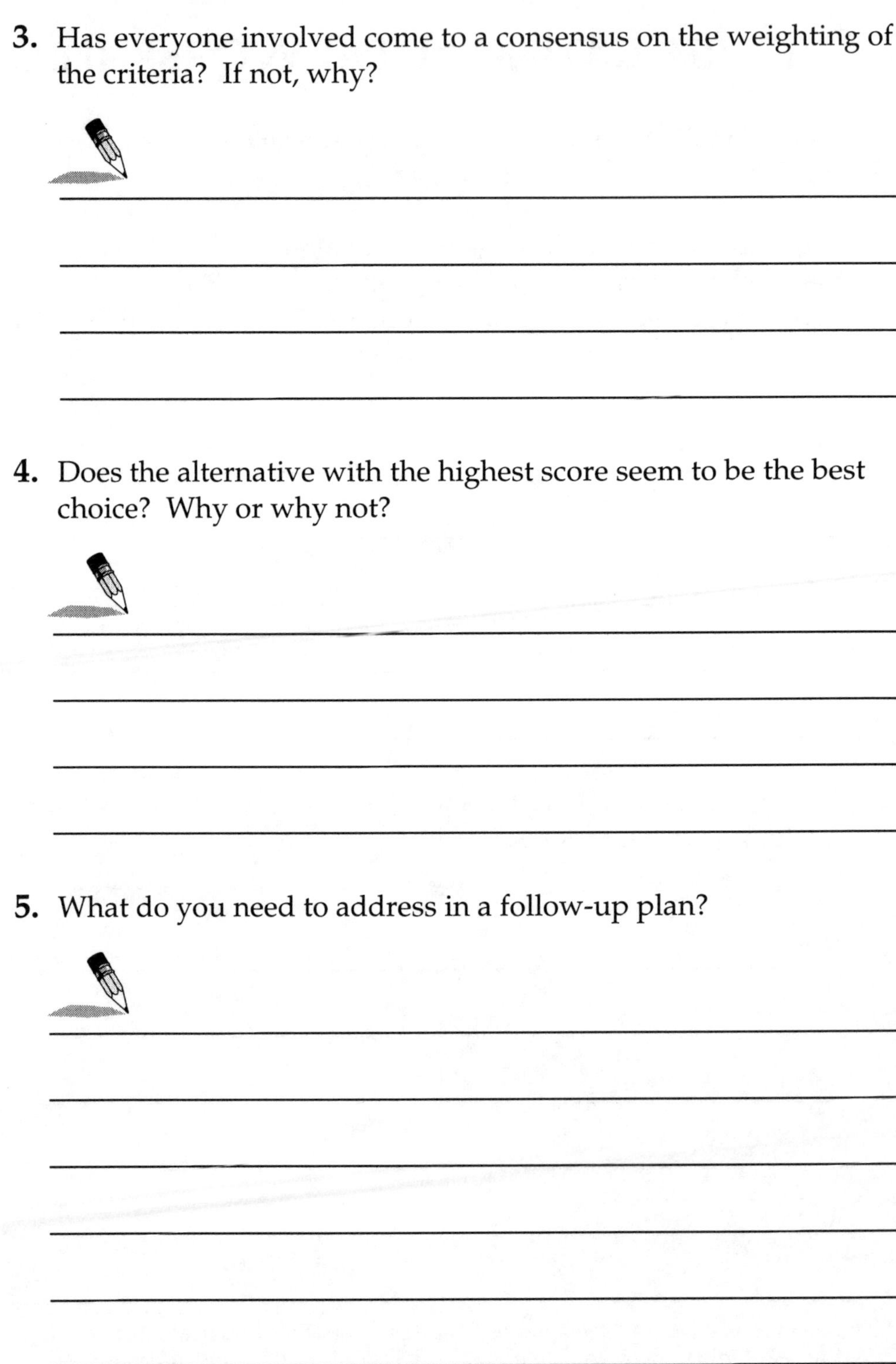

4. Does the alternative with the highest score seem to be the best choice? Why or why not?

5. What do you need to address in a follow-up plan?

CRITERIA RATING FORM

		ALTERNATIVES		
Criteria	Weight			
Total				
Summary				

CHECK SHEET WORKSHEET

Address the following questions when preparing to use the Check Sheet:

1. Are others, who may be affected, aware of why you are gathering information and how it will be used?

2. Identify what information you will gather.

3. How will you compare this information to information from other time periods?

4. How will you interpret the data on the Check Sheet *(e.g., by using a Pareto Chart)*?

5. How will you communicate the data and the conclusions drawn from it?

CHECK SHEET

							Total
Total							

NOTES

NOTES

NOTES

NOTES

NOTES

NOTES

- W/W come our school to be #1

organization   performance

       Leadership

- W/ Leadership qualities are needed to

get from A — Z ?

Org   +   perform.

- How can we effectively plan for

Success? Key flows Areas

A. scheduling 1 — 10 enhancer / detractor

- How do we move from this to this be?

- note Covey   +

- Brainstorming, Affinity Diagram, etc.

(#) - Leadership Profile